The Chartists

A Socialist History of Britain

Series edited by the Northern Marxist Historians Group

The Chartists

The First National Workers' Movement

John Charlton

Pluto Press

LONDON · CHICAGO, ILLINOIS

322.2
C48c

First published 1997 by Pluto Press
345 Archway Road, London N6 5AA
and 1436 West Randolph
Chicago, Illinois 60607, USA

British Library Cataloguing in Publication Data
A catalogue record for this book is available from the British
Library

ISBN   0 7453 1182 2 hbk

Library of Congress Cataloging in Publication Data
Charlton, John, 1938–
     The Chartists: the first national workers' movement/John
Charlton.
          p.   cm. — (Socialist history of Britain)
     Includes bibliographical references and index.
     ISBN 0–7453–1182–2
     1. Chartism. 2. Labor movement—Great Britain—History-
-19th century.   I. Title. II. Series.
     HD8396.C48   1997
     322'.2'0941—dc20   96–34396
JK   CIP

2001 2000 1999 1998 1997 5 4 3 2 1

Designed and produced for Pluto Press by
Chase Production Services, Chadlington, OX7 3LN
Typeset by Stanford DTP Services, Milton Keynes
Printed in the EC by J.W. Arrowsmith Ltd, Bristol, England

Contents

For Roy Charlton

Acknowledgements

My thanks must go first to the dozens of authors more expert than me whose work I have looted to produce this book. Of course it is a tribute to the importance of the Chartists that so many writers have sought to uncover the tiniest part of their story. It is now possible to find accounts of the movement in almost all regions of Britain, to read biographies of all the main figures and some of the minor ones, and to learn about the language, the dress codes and symbols and the activities of teetotal Chartists, Chartist educators, Christian Chartists, Chartist trade unionists, Chartists in America, Irish Chartists, Chartist prisoners and female Chartists. Less anonymously, I have to thank Mike Haynes, David McNally, Raymond Challinor, Mick Charlton, Keith Flett, Donnie Gluckstein, Sally Mitchison and, above all, John Saville.

Introduction

Between 1838 and 1848 the Chartist movement drew thousands of people into political activity. Some of its national leaders and most of its local leaders were working men. Its mass circulation weekly newspaper, the *Northern Star,* speaking consistently to workers' concerns, had a massive working-class readership. Many of its local groups, reaching towards party organisation, drew on the experience of trade unionism. In its moments of maximum impact, in 1839, 1842 and 1848, it mobilised hundreds of thousands of workers, uniting spinners, weavers, miners, engineers, farm labourers, bricklayers, carpenters, navvies, seamen, dockers, tailors, shoemakers, blacksmiths and printers. The victims of the state's vengeance against the movement – those imprisoned and those transported – were overwhelmingly working-class. Chartism was the first national workers' movement in history.

In the second quarter of the nineteenth century the problems brought by industrialisation were bearing very heavily upon workers' lives. The domestic system of production in many industries was in its death throes and its remaining workers were suffering rapidly declining living standards. The refugees of the handicraft sector joined displaced farm workers and Irish immigrants in servicing the new factories, iron-works and coal-mines. In the new factory sector, operatives faced working days of up to 18 hours for barely subsistence wages. They were subjected to brutal discipline in extremely inhospitable surroundings – mere 'hands' to manipulate the expanding and unsafe world of machines. The widespread employment of children, from five years of age, robbed them of their childhood and contributed to a life expectancy, for some groups, of as low as the late teens.

These work people were sucked into a new urban environment of almost unspeakable horror. Hurriedly built ramshackle 'cottages' and the wet and lightless cellars of tenement blocks served as billets for the new arrivals. Devoid of heating, cooking facilities and adequate sanitation, such buildings sometimes sat beneath the factory walls, repositories of overcrowding, domestic and community violence, and rampant disease.

It was workers from such milieux who formed the shock troops of the burgeoning mass movements of 1839, 1842 and 1848. They joined with artisans and members of the lower middle class, many of whom were the carriers of a long tradition of English working-class radicalism. This was a tradition stretching back into the eighteenth century and one which had made serial, but temporary, contact with the plebeian masses. It was a tradition which had been given direction and vitality in the 1790s in the acute polarities of response to the great French Revolution. The Corresponding Societies, in proclaiming their desire for 'members unlimited', carried political discourse far beyond the usual social groups, taking up and transmitting the hard egalitarian politics of Thomas Paine.

Their successors enthusiastically embraced a myriad of ideas: from Thomas Spence, the idea of public ownership of land; from Robert Owen, a restructuring of society along communitarian lines and all-embracing trade unionism; from Thomas Hodgkin and others, a socialism based on the labour theory of value; and from William Cobbett, a devastating attack on 'Old Corruption' and the values of industrial society.

Imbued with an array of anti-establishment ideologies, working-class radicals moved into a series of campaigns, in some of them engaging with a mass of workers beyond their ranks. There were Short Time Committees, the gigantic and bitter opposition to the New Poor Law, the fight to establish a free radical press, and the angry struggle to free the Tolpuddle Martyrs and the Glasgow Cotton Spinners. Running through the whole period, often just beneath the surface, then breaking out into mass action, was the demand for franchise reform. The Peterloo Massacre of 1819, which occurred in the course of one such campaign, was an indelible reminder of the system's inequality and injustice. Working men and women had risen to the banner of parliamentary reform again between 1830 and 1832, only to be sharply reminded of their exclusion with the Reform Act of 1832. In a decade of rising tensions, social, economic and political, the drawing up and publishing of the People's Charter in 1838 proved to be the catalyst for pent-up frustrations. The six points were expressly political. The movement they inspired was much more. As Engels noted in *The Condition of the Working Class in England in 1844*, Chartism was 'of an essentially social nature, a class movement':

> The 'Six Points' which for the radical bourgeoisie are the beginning and end of the matter, which are meant, at the utmost, to call forth certain further reforms of the Constitution, are for the proletarian, a mere means to further ends. 'Political power our means, social happiness our end' is now the clearly formulated war-cry of the Chartists. The 'knife and fork' question of the preacher Stephen was a truth for a part of the Chartists only, in 1838; it is a truth for all of them in 1845.

The character and potential of Chartism was also noted by the ruling class. Law and order had long been a preoccupation of the rulers. Presiding over such stark inequality, with tiny numbers benefiting from privilege, complacency could have been utter folly. The extreme brutality and savagery of the judicial system had been tailored to deal with a largely rural society peppered with small towns, though London had always raised additional problems. The key issues had been poaching, smuggling, excise avoidance, petty theft, indigence and the occasional (and usually brief) urban riot. The new industrial society threw up strikes, mass strikes, mass demonstrations, insurrection and lasting political movements of dissent. These manifestations were all part of Chartism. The response was a growing concentration of the forces of the state to curb, contain, then destroy the perceived threat to existing property relations.

The workers' movement was vigorous and tenacious. It rose three times, in 1839, 1842 and in 1848. In the latter year it was defeated and broken by a concerted and ordered offensive from the new capitalist state. It was over 40 years before an independent movement of working people was able to re-establish itself.

CHAPTER 1

The 1830s – Bourgeois Power and the Working Class

By the 1840s industrial capitalism had more than a half century of growth. Industrial villages had long been sprouting in the North, the Midlands, South Wales and the Clyde Valley. Displaced rural workers had been drawn into burgeoning towns like Manchester, Liverpool, Birmingham, Sheffield, Leeds, Bradford and Glasgow. The 1851 Census was the first to register a majority of the population as town-dwellers. New technologies and new forms of work organisation had been eroding skill. In the 1830s and 1840s there was a proliferation of descriptive commentaries and analyses by writers like Frederick Engels, Peter Gaskell, Andrew Ure, James Kaye, Edward Baines, Leon Faucher, John Fielden, William Cooke Taylor, Charles Babbage and Charles Dickens and many minor figures. Whether triumphalist, critical or merely anxious, they indicate that middle-class contemporaries were aware of a massive acceleration of change in their own lifetimes. Their work often exudes a sense of cataclysm:

> From Birmingham to Wolverhampton, a distance of thirteen miles, the country was curious and amusing; though not very pleasing to eyes, ears or taste; for part of it seemed a sort of pandemonium on earth – a region of smoke and fire filling the whole earth between earth and heaven; amongst which certain figures of human shape – if shape they had – were seen occasionally to glide from one cauldron of curling flame to another ...[1]

In the 1830s the industrial revolution entered a serious crisis. The transfusion to be offered by the revolution in metal-working and the railway frenzy was still around the corner. The canal-building and textile booms of the previous 60 years were tumbling into ever-deepening recessions. After 1815, no longer cushioned by the demand of a war economy, the domestic system of textile manufacture was in terminal crisis.

Middle-class observers could be moved by anger at what they saw of the new industrial system but they *were* just observers. Working people were at the system's centre; the creators of its wealth.

Exploitation and oppression were the very heart of the process. Workers could only attain a subsistence wage by toiling for up to 16 hours per day. Women and children might be paid less than subsistence wages because they were readily available and not perceived as the family's main wage earner. Conditions at work were dismal with no attention being paid to safety or workers' health. An authoritarian management imposed rigid rules of conduct punishable by fines and summary dismissal, backed by the Master and Servants Law of 1823.

For most working people recession was a way of life. By 1850, a 40-year-old worker could have experienced no fewer than seven depressions (1819, 1826, 1829, 1832, 1837, 1842 and 1848). Downturns in trade accelerated the pace of technical and organisational change. Employers fought to gain autonomy over the labour process. Most trades were affected. In cotton, the domestic system had been virtually marginalised by the end of the eighteenth century. From the 1820s the fight was on to install the self-acting mule to allow greater concentration of production and a further erosion of skill. Concentration was rapid in wool, as handicrafts located in homes were replaced by central workshops. Semi-independent weavers, woolcombers, stockingers and laceworkers in Yorkshire and Nottinghamshire were decimated, their earnings catastrophically reduced in the 30 years following the end of the war. The woolworkers of East Anglia and the South West were virtually wiped out. Metalworkers and potters in the West Midlands were subjected to fiercer and fiercer market pressures by middlemen and the intrusion of large-scale manufacturers. Even the most skilled trades like printing, bookbinding, watch and gun-making, carpentry, coach-building and mill-wrighting were subjected to the pressures of dilution, as Parliament excised ancient protective legislation on entry, apprenticeship and quality control. London artisans had fought on this ground for over 50 years. These were secular trends intensified in the depression years.

This viciously subordinate relationship at work was truly reflected in the workers' situation beyond the factory, workshop and mine. Home was frequently an overcrowded hovel, offering little protection from the elements, a repository of violence, disease and death. The streets, teeming with people, were fraught with danger from arbitrary violence, pollution from factory chimneys, stagnant pools, mineshafts and germs from running sewers, graphically described by Engels in *The Condition of the Working Class in England in 1844:*

> At the bottom flows, or rather stagnates, the Irk, a narrow, coal-black, foul smelling stream, full of debris and refuse ... In dry weather, a long string of the most disgusting, blackish-green, slime pools are left standing on this bank, from the depths of

which bubbles of miasmatic gas constantly arise and give forth
a stench unendurable even on the bridge forty or fifty feet above
the surface of the stream ... the stream itself is checked every
few paces by high weirs, behind which slime and refuse
accumulate and rot in thick masses ... Above the bridge are
tanneries, bonemills, and gasworks, from which all drains and
refuse find their way into the Irk which receives the contents of
all the neighbouring sewers and privies ... Below the bridge you
look upon the piles of debris, the refuse, filth and offal from the
courts on the steep left bank.

A few public-spirited physicians laboured in the squalor, fighting
fruitless battles against epidemics. Diarrhoea was the biggest killer,
its number of victims incalculable. Tuberculosis killed 59,000 in
1838 alone. Whooping cough accounted for 10,000 deaths annually
and measles 7000. Even minor injuries could result in incapacity
or death.

Despite the ravages of the cholera epidemic which struck urban
Britain in 1831, killing 30,000 people, the 1830s opened with a
glimmer of hope. Buoyed by news of revolution in Europe, a
movement for reform of Parliament re-emerged. Hundreds of
thousands of workers were propelled into political activity organised
by middle-class and artisan Political Unions. This movement was
strongest in Birmingham, Manchester and Leeds, but the flashpoints
were Nottingham, Bristol and, most dramatically, Merthyr Tydfil,
where the workers temporarily ruled the town. These upsurges were
produced by spontaneous crowd alliances in which trade boundaries
and skilled/unskilled boundaries melted into the air.

The events of Merthyr were not part of the pressure for reform
promoted by the middle class; they represented the most insurrectionary act of the new working class so far. In Merthyr the
stresses of nascent capitalism reached breaking point at the end of
May 1831. An early coal and iron boom town, it was a magnet for
the poor rural Welsh and those from further afield. In two decades
the settlement had mushroomed into the largest town in Wales.
In the general national crisis the specific problems of Merthyr
raised unrest to the level of insurrection as ironworkers and miners
took on proprietors, shopocracy and army, holding the town for
four days and providing Wales with its first working-class martyr,
Dic Penderyn. He was tried and hanged, largely for being in the
right place at the wrong time.

The insurrection failed to spread to neighbouring communities,
giving the military time to regroup to defeat the workers.
Nevertheless, the crucible of insurrection clearly sharpened class
attitudes and created a class consciousness quickly reflected in the
lightening spread of trade unionism across the valleys of eastern

Wales. Short-lived though this was, crushed by a determined employers' offensive, the class-conscious sentiments created were revived at the end of the decade in the Chartist Newport Rising.

In 1830 Nottingham and Bristol turned out to be the centres of a mass involvement for reform not reached elsewhere. Timid middle-class leadership advised, even fought for caution. Artisan exclusivity still handicapped the coherence of the movement, especially in London. Crucially, the ruling class made the minimum concession necessary to consolidate the alliance between land and industry and commerce. The character of politics for the next two decades was set in the Reform Act settlement of 1832 and the Municipal Corporation Act which followed in 1835.

The Reform Act has sometimes been seen as minimalist legislation. In terms of the *number* of new electors this may be true, but such a view is to miss its real significance. It is no exaggeration to argue that it may have been the single most important piece of legislation of the nineteenth century. It placed a ring around the middle class and linked them emphatically to the ruling order. That it was not complete, that the middle class continued to supply dissent on a wide range of questions, is beside the point. From 1832, the bulk of the middle class was a reliably conservative social force.

The franchise was widened to include all men of sufficient property. The balance of representation shifted from south to north, embracing the manufacturing districts. The industrial towns were the main beneficiaries. Any shortcomings for the middle class in the 1832 Act were compensated for in the Municipal Corporations Act of 1835. They dominated the towns. Political power was added to economic and social power.

Increasingly working people in these towns were to face the bourgeoisie or their agents directly. Inequality and class bias were scored into the very highways. Enormous municipal extravagance in the shape of grand public buildings celebrating bourgeois values were to be erected alongside, or on the site of, workers' slums. Elegant stone-built mansions arose in carefully delineated middle-class districts whilst workers' housing was thrown up in the path of the smoke of factory chimneys. Neo-Gothic churches and chapels were erected to save men's souls whilst their bodies were left to suffer in mill and mine.

A precarious peace was preserved. The middle classes built bridges to the upper strata of the working class through encouraging chapel attendance, membership of friendly societies and the co-operative movement. A new police force was founded and plentifully supplemented at times of crisis by young men of the middle class dressed as policemen – the special constables.

The new ruling-class alliance gave a stronger framework to the implementation of political economy. Working people were

persistently faced by the strident claim that *laissez-faire* was the natural
state of affairs. Even the most modest proposal for factory reform
was opposed on the grounds that it would fatally disturb the natural
workings of the market. This included shorter working hours and
limitations on the employment of child labour. Such theoretical
purity would be breached by the rulers when convenient. The
blunt instruments of state power could be invoked to prevent
workers' combination and regulate the lives of the poor.

Nowhere was this seen more clearly in the 1830s than in the Poor
Law Amendment Act of 1834. After 30 years of anxiety, indeed
hysteria, at the rising cost of the old Poor Law, which dated back
to the Tudor period, Parliament established a Commission of
Enquiry in 1832 to examine it and to make recommendations.
Paradoxically, perhaps, ruling-class pressure for reform of the
system came at a point when the cost was actually falling. A clue
to motivation is offered by a rural magistrate, writing to Sir Robert
Peel after the rural riots of 1830. He claimed that, 'if this state of
things should continue the Peasantry will learn the secret of their
own strength'.[2] A dose of firm discipline was what was required.

Under the direction of Edwin Chadwick, a pioneering middle-
class utilitarian administrator, a report was produced which exposed
the existing system in a way which drew special attention to a
range of problems central to capitalist production. These were,
specifically, the Poor Law's alleged tendency to distort the labour
market, cut down labour mobility, restrict the 'freedom' of labourers
to sell their labour, to distort the wages system, to demoralise
labour and to threaten public order. The remedies were to abandon
outdoor relief and to create 'less eligibility'. By establishing an
alternative system of relief in institutions – workhouses – in which
conditions were more onerous than could be found outside, it was
hoped that the poor would be driven to accept work at the market
price. Implicit, too, was a fierce attack on the independence of
women. On the assumption that women were completely dependent
upon their spouses, unmarried women were forced into the
workhouse, yet in reality working-class women were often the
main breadwinners. By placing the emphasis firmly upon the
responsibility of the male to provide for the family (a test of his
masculinity), two pieces of ideology were implanted: the subservience
of women and moral turpitude associated with asking the state for
assistance.

The New Poor Law was immediately felt as crude class legislation
by working people. Since it was replacing a law born of a paternalistic
system and a parliament of landed interests, it was seen as the work
of the middle class, the 'traitors of 32'. As the main employers of
waged labour they, ad most to gain. Certain classes of outworkers,
and the weavers and woolcombers in particular, were in an advanced

state of decline; the woolcombers were 'a sort of common reservoir of all the poverty of England and Ireland'.[3] The new law promised to bear very heavily upon them and their families. Factory workers were becoming used to the effects of the boom–slump cycle. Slumps and unemployment were likely to throw them on the mercy of this new law.

The law was first enacted in the southern counties where agricultural labourers were demoralised by the crushing reaction which followed the Swing riots in 1830 and their failure to save the Tolpuddle Martyrs in 1834. Despite considerable resistance the workhouse building programme was carried out and the Act was in place by 1837. As attention turned to the industrial Midlands and the North a deep depression hit trade in 1837. A massive campaign of resistance to the law developed in the factory districts – most intensely in south-east Lancashire, where a genuine across-trades mass workers' movement developed. An outstanding leader of this activity was Joseph Rayner Stephens, a Methodist minister, who was to be a central figure in the first stage of Lancashire Chartism and who saw Chartism as 'a knife and fork question'.[4] One result of militant agitation was that it took over 15 years to implement the New Poor Law in Lancashire and even then only in modified form.

Anti-Poor Law activity was not the first working-class campaign to follow the suffrage agitation. Short Time Committees had been formed in 1831 to campaign for factory reform. They proliferated in West Yorkshire and the Manchester district, holding large assemblies and organising mass petitions. Although they had achieved only modest success with the Factory Acts of 1834, their members and organisation flowed into the Anti-Poor Law agitation.[5] Furthermore, working-class men and women were deeply involved in the agitations to save the agricultural labourers of Tolpuddle in 1834 and the Glasgow Cotton Spinners in 1837, both crude attacks by the state on incipient trade unionism. Many were to move on to become a critical organisational foundation of Chartism, especially in the industrial districts.

Spearheaded by the *Poor Man's Guardian*, a virtual underground organisation existed to produce and circulate radical newspapers in defiance of the Act banning an unstamped press.[6] This was a struggle which reached back decades. It was interwoven with other strands in the development of radicalism: the belligerent anti-establishment journalism and pamphleteering of Thomas Paine and William Cobbett, Mary Wollstonecraft and women's rights, the demand for suffrage, republicanism, religious toleration and free-thinking, workers' education, anti-slavery campaigns, and anti-corruption in government. Artisan involvement dated from post-Civil War attempts to organise the London trades and the development of a rich and vibrant cultural tradition around London pubs and coffee houses.

In the 1790s such impulses had taken on clear organisational form in the emergence of the Corresponding Societies. Identifying with the *sans culottes* of revolutionary Paris but imbued with the vigorous English radicalism of Thomas Paine, the Societies became the first political organisations of working men inviting 'members unlimited'. Their growth and activity in the early years of the war with France was a major cause of the assembling, by William Pitt, of a new repressive state apparatus in that decade. Driven from the streets into an opaque underground, many of these activists survived to carry and pass on their experience to future generations of radicals.

The acquisition of literacy, the solidity of organisational practices, the resistance to state interference, persistent threats to their skill, the mounting of a long and intelligent critique of the precepts of political economy and the sheer obduracy of the democratic tradition made the artisans a potent source for the founding and promotion of the Charter.

CHAPTER 2

The Making of the Charter

A national campaign

Of all the issues which fed into the movement for suffrage extension the campaign against the stamp duty on newspapers was the most immediate because its centre was London where most papers were published. The persistence of its participants, over decades, had established an organisation on the ground with hundreds of activists and, crucially, a determined and articulate leadership. In addition to older or more experienced men like Cobbett, who died in 1835, Richard Carlile, who had suffered repeated prison sentences, and Henry Hetherington, proprietor of the *Poor Man's Guardian*, a new layer of figures including William Lovett, Bronterre O'Brien and Julian Harney cut their political teeth in this struggle.

In 1835 the government, under pressure, reduced the stamp duty, whilst intensifying repression. But this move perhaps simply whetted an appetite for struggle. The gathering together in London of leading campaigners to take the contest forward resulted in the founding of the London Working Men's Association in the summer of 1836. There was already a belief among even moderate radicals that little could be expected of the reformed Parliament. Indeed a major architect of the Reform Act, Lord John Russell, had declared that the British Constitution was now perfect and in need of no further amendment. However, five general elections in the short period since the Reform Act had maintained political interest and excitement, and a climate in which reformers could raise the demand for suffrage reform as the only means to bring about broader reform.

The outcome was the formulation, by the London Working Men's Association in January 1837, of an address to Parliament embodying the six points of what was to be known as 'The People's Charter': universal suffrage, no property qualifications, annual parliaments, equal representation, payment of MPs, and vote by ballot. There is a perhaps arcane controversy over its authorship, although it should be noted that it apparently circulated in the provinces before the final version was drafted. Was it William Lovett or Francis Place?[1] Whoever's pen it was, Place's influence is apparent, directly or indirectly. He was the great survivor of radical

11

politics, his activity reaching back to the London Corresponding Society of the 1790s. For more than 30 years he had occupied a 'wire pulling'[2] world between London artisans and radical (and not so radical) Westminster politics. It was a world in which he had developed close relations with the philosophical radicals, especially Jeremy Bentham, James Mill and Joseph Hume. He was a strong advocate of political economy and hostile to Owenism and other variations of socialist theory. It is significant that the Charter avoided points which emanate from the labour theory of value, unlike, for example, the Declaration of the National Union of the Working Classes drafted by William Lovett in 1831 and headed 'Labour is the Source of Wealth'. On the other hand, it is difficult to see how a campaign launched with the connivance of six named middle-class radical MPs could have used a form of words which included the sphere of socio-economic reform. That would have been anathema to their liberal beliefs. So what emerged was a document which in both content and language resembled earlier formulations of parliamentary reform going back to the 1780s. How it would be understood by the very different social elements which were to swing behind it was a very different matter.

In the spring of 1837 the London reformers sent missionaries throughout Britain to encourage the fledgling reform movement. Over the following 18 months remarkable mass meetings were held in many places, including a reported 200,000 on Glasgow Green and over 100,000 each on Hartshead Moor (West Yorkshire) and Kersal Moor (near Manchester). The Political Unions of the Reform Bill agitation were revived in Birmingham, Manchester, Newcastle, Leeds and Scotland, all demonstrating a massive groundswell of popular support for the principles of the Charter.

The revived Birmingham Political Union advocated the organising of a mass petition to Parliament. It was a compromise tactic adopted after negotiations between the Birmingham and London radicals. The tactic belonged to an earlier radical tradition. Its weaknesses were widely understood and much commented upon. Each of the three rounds undertaken were looked upon by many as 'the last'. Militants saw it quite clearly as a deliberate diversion from direct action.

One of the most significant things about Chartism was that it was a national movement. Given the uneven development of the economy and hence that of the working class, it is remarkable that a movement should emerge with such a universal following in Britain. However part of the process of understanding is in the exploration of the disparate local threads which coalesced around the Charter.

Local roots

London Chartism was the political manifestation of the London artisan trade societies. In being for a long time, they had formed the backbone of Jacobinism in the 1790s, and had, to a large extent, survived the years of repression whilst the war against France lasted. Engaged in the campaign to defend apprenticeship and the suffrage struggle after the war, they had led or participated in the major political campaigns of the 1820s: in embarrassing the government in the Queen Caroline Affair,[3] agitating for repeal of the Combination Acts and for the establishment of Benefit Societies.

In the 1830s they had moved again into suffrage issues and the campaigns to free the Tolpuddle Martyrs and the Glasgow Cotton Spinners.[4] Providing the linkage between areas and campaigns and organisations were dozens of newspapers and pamphlets. Their journalists and sellers behaved with extraordinary courage in the face of enormous intimidation by the state authorities using taxation of publications as the lever to try to drive dissent off the streets. The determination of figures like Henry Hetherington, Thomas Wooler, Richard Carlile, Alan Davenport, Bronterre O'Brien and a multitude of 'unknown' street sellers, brought the law into disrepute by their persistence in risking arrest and suffering prison sentences.[5] The government's reduction of newspaper tax, dubbed by radicals the 'tax on knowledge' was of vital importance to the role played by the Chartist press in the following decade.

By the 1830s London radicals also had two generations of solid trade union activity behind them, an activity requiring determination in very exacting circumstances. Some had reached out, albeit tentatively, to Owenite general unionism. Their political organisation, however, the London Working Men's Association, reflected their craft unionism. They were generous in commitment to political campaigns but exclusive, refusing to embrace the exploited poor of south and east London, and tactically cautious, in pursuit of 'the intelligent and influential portion of the working classes in town and country'. Exclusivity, determination and caution was what they brought to Chartism, personified by their leading light, William Lovett.[6]

There was another wing of Chartism in London. The attitudes of this artisan culture were anathema to a political stratum rooted in Jacobinism, Spenceite and Owenite socialism and the propagation of a sharp and distinctive working-class interest. Commencing in the East End, the East London Democratic Association drew from the ranks of poorer working men including the marginalised silkweavers of Spitalfield. Founded in 1837, they were soon in conflict with the London Working Men's Association on a number of issues, including a defence of trade unionism, the need to embrace an insurrectionary strategy and the possibility of working with middle-class radicals in pursuit of suffrage reform.[7]

Workers in the London trades had been engaged in a bitter struggle going back more than 50 years. To a considerable extent the oppositionist culture noted above was born and nurtured in a cauldron of attempts to reduce wages, remove traditional perquisites, the displacement of men by machinery, the growth of injurious practices at work, pressure to introduce 'illegal' men and extra apprentices, the introduction of piecework and subcontracting, and the introduction and expansion of domestic sweated labour. Working people in the world's oldest industrial economy were in the front line of a fundamental process of capital restructuring. They resisted and fought back on many fronts. The battle for the Charter created a potent focus.

Like London, Birmingham was a city of small craft workshops. The industrial revolution had meant a proliferation of tiny workshops and there were very few substantial factories. Such enterprises produced considerable social fluidity, since workers usually saw their well-being in upward movement. The father of Birmingham Chartism, the banker, Thomas Attwood, saw political association as a tool of class collaboration:

> The interests of masters and men are in fact one. If the masters flourish, the men are certain to flourish with them; if the masters suffer difficulties, their difficulties must shortly affect the workmen in a threefold degree. The masters therefore ought to take their workmen by the hand and knock at the gates of government and demand the redress of their common grievances.[8]

A policy based on these sentiments had enjoyed some success in the Reform Bill agitation, the Birmingham Political Union having taken the lead in that struggle. However, its high-middle-class profile had held it back from supporting many of the radical campaigns of the 1830s and its composition and outlooks were to prove a severe handicap in an alliance where the working class carried a good deal more organisational, as well as numerical weight. Nonetheless, these problems were not to surface immediately and Birmingham men played a central part in launching the Chartist movement, even to the point of advocating and sponsoring the first Convention in 1839.

The movement in south-east Lancashire shared some of the preoccupations of the London and Birmingham movements. Manchester had been a centre of suffrage campaigns since the 1790s and Lancashire was the focal point of such activity which had culminated in Peterloo in the years following the war. The Manchester Political Union was active in the Reform Bill crisis but there had been an increasing tendency for divergence between middle- and working-class radicalism. In Oldham the working class, confident and strident, had been intimidating bourgeois and petit bourgeois for a generation. It had actually succeeding in getting its 'appointees' into positions of control, including, incredibly, the Police Committee. It has been argued that the Oldham working class, in the mid-1830s, reached the highest form of class consciousness experienced anywhere in the British Isles in the nineteenth century.[9] It cannot, however, be said that Oldham played a leading role in north-west Chartism, even at the peak of working-class involvement in 1842.

From the late 1830s, the middle classes had steered firmly away from the suffrage issue to Corn Law repeal; indeed the Manchester bourgeoisie was unquestionably the leading pressure group in that national campaign. This reflected its position as a manufacturing ruling class dedicated to the pursuit of free trade. The paternalism inherent in the small master–artisan relationship was long since gone in much of Lancashire industry, to be replaced by an unambiguous profile of class domination. After the publication of the Charter, the mouthpiece of Whiggism, the *Manchester Guardian,* poured scorn on its demands:

> Annual Parliaments ... would only increase 'the expense, the trouble, and the turmoil of electioneering'; payment of members would bring 'the lucre of private gain' into politics; and universal suffrage would give the vote 'to every drunkard and blackguard in the kingdom'. The suffrage was not a right as the Chartists claimed: 'it is merely an expedient for obtaining good government; *that,* and not the franchise, it is to which the public have a right.'[10]

This was the ideological context for Lancashire Chartism and the working class responded with a militancy at times swinging into insurrectionist *intention,* if not achievement. Unlike London, where the movement was run and dominated by the upper strata of artisans and radical intelligentsia, the Lancashire movement was broad-based, bringing into activity workers from a multitude of trades and occupations.[11] It has been suggested that the only significant working groups actually missing were the markedly better-off craftsmen, 'printers, bookbinders and coachmakers', and, contrary to a formerly accepted belief, 'significant numbers of the more advantaged, aristocratically inclined, engineering and metalworking trades' were present.[12] Lancashire Chartism had all the character of a mass workers' movement illustrated by the enormous turnouts from the industrial towns on the great demonstrations[13] and especially by the now established connections between the Chartist organisation and leaders and the great strike waves of the summer of 1842.

The situation in Yorkshire was complex. Leeds was a town of large mills and small workshops where handloom weaving had already been squeezed out, though this was not the case in the myriad of small industrial villages which surrounded it. Like Manchester it had long radical traditions and activists but they had fallen out with the middle-class radicals even before the Reform Bill crisis. The leadership of Leeds radicalism, therefore, already had a more working-class composition and orientation. It had a militancy and solidity which certainly attracted Feargus O'Connor who launched the *Northern Star* from Leeds in 1837, giving the town a very early and specific association with the movement.

Bradford was very different. In a town that had grown explosively with class relations to match, an insurrectionary tendency was prominent, reflecting the desperate plight of the weavers and woolcombers whose living standards had plummeted with the introduction of the power loom and combing machinery in the 1830s and 1840s. A hard proletarian consciousness prevailed with the formation of weavers' and combers' unions following a major strike in 1825 and the launching of the national Ten Hours Movement. The town was also a centre of the anti-Poor Law campaign; after a riot in 1837 the Poor Law commissioners postponed implementation. When they did implement it later in the year, the crowds fought the police and soldiers. The support for militant activities given by the *Northern Star* was probably the catalyst which brought Bradford swinging into the new movement.

There were two main centres of activity in South Yorkshire: Sheffield and Barnsley. The former, slower to move initially, was a town predominantly of artisans in a myriad of small metal workshops, but as a substantial regional centre there was also a sizeable middle class with a radical wing. This placed Sheffield Chartism near to the Birmingham pattern, though there was also a small Jacobin culture, which ran back to the 1790s. The Sheffield Corresponding Society had published a 6d edition of *The Rights of Man*, Part 1, in 1791, and claimed several thousand adherents. After the failure of the great petition in 1839 the 'Jacobins' dragged the local movement towards insurrection.[14] Barnsley, with a substantial linen industry in decline, a growing coal-mining industry, and a small middle class, had a more proletarian and militant cast throughout the 1820s and 1830s, traditions which were to motivate local Chartism from the start.[15]

Tyneside Chartism also grew out of the Reform struggle in which the Northern Political Union had played a leading role. In Newcastle, a major regional centre of trade and finance, the middle classes had been central to radical politics, but by 1838 there was considerable antagonism. Some of the key reformers of 1832 were, by then, city aldermen. The best radical regional newspaper of the time, the *Northern Liberator*, was widely read across the region, acting as an effective propagandist and organiser. It helped to bring into the movement the powerful presence of ironworkers and colliers from outlying villages where Jacobinism was alive and workers were reputedly armed. A leading organiser, Thomas Ainge Devyr, claimed that 'from [August 1838] to November we computed sixty thousand pikes made and shafted on the Tyne and Wear'.[16] It was into an already excited atmosphere that Julian Harney arrived, in the winter of 1838, to speak on Christmas Day to a crowd on the Town Moor of up to 80,000.

Scottish and Welsh Chartism form contrasting pictures, the former marked, largely, by its moderation and the latter by its revolutionary intent. Although dozens of Chartist groups developed in Scotland, the origins of Scottish Chartism were in the centres of Glasgow and Edinburgh, both focal points of radicalism from the late eighteenth century. In common with much English radicalism, movements were usually led by members of the middle classes, but, like Leeds and Manchester, a cross-class alliance was placed under severe strain in the 1830s, both by the accelerated growth of working-class activity and by certain key middle-class radicals' hostile attitudes to trade union activity. The issue of the Glasgow Cotton Spinners provoked rage among the workers, whilst some Whiggish radicals (notably Daniel O'Connell) sided with the state, even to the extent of calling for an enquiry into the activities of workers' combinations. O'Connell became an obvious target for Feargus O'Connor who had already, by 1836, embarked on his gruelling speaking tours, including Scotland, where he had appeared at a mass rally on Glasgow Green in December. Despite a move to the left, the lower middle class of shopkeepers, attorneys and journalists, with cottonworkers, colliers and the usual complement of shoemakers, did not move far beyond 'constitutional' methods of protest.

In its origins Welsh Chartism had a strong non-conformist background although there were small numbers of free-thinkers too. Radicalism in Wales had flourished in the 1820s and during the Reform Bill agitation but hostile divisions between Whigs and radicals had soon developed, mainly over the degree to which radicals wished to push a social programme stressing class differences. Some of the early key figures had associations with Lovett and the London Working Men's Association. Two of the three earliest centres, Carmarthen and Merthyr, were strongly 'moral force' in their leanings and a third, Montgomeryshire, rapidly shifted from that position to militant action in the flannel-weaving town of Llanidloes in late April 1839.

Moderate delegates were sent from Wales to the Convention, supporting the national petition, but when it was rejected, the working-class membership in the coal and iron-working valleys above Newport swept into the movement in thousands and arming commenced. Despite his misgivings, the Newport linen draper and magistrate, John Frost, himself a moderate, placed himself at the head of the movement which in the autumn moved into rebellion with a mass march upon Newport. South Wales Chartism had become, by mid-1839, a thoroughly proletarian movement.

There were Chartist followers in most other parts of the British Isles, from the old declining woollen districts of the South West, to urban and rural East Anglia, south-west Scotland and even Ireland. The central core of adherents in most areas had long political genealogies running as far back as the 1790s. Together they brought to the movement a variegated set of ideas: Jacobin, Paineite, Spenceite, Cobbettite, Owenite and a range of dissenting and free-thinking philosophical standpoints. Although, as a general rule, the social composition of the earliest local sections tended to be lower middle class and 'superior' artisans, by the time of the national petition's presentation in the spring of 1839, the movement was overwhelmingly working class, embracing both skilled and unskilled men and women. It was at its numerically strongest in the leading industrial areas where it was most militant too.

1839, The Convention ...

A polarisation of strategies was apparent, with a section of the London movement and workers in the industrial Midlands and North advancing more militant and vigorous action in support of the demands than either the middle-class leaders of the Political Unions or the leadership of the London artisans. A Northern Union had been launched by Feargus O'Connor. Recently disqualified from Parliament, to which he had been elected from County Cork in the election of 1835, he had found the artisan-radical culture of London stifling. He sought a much broader canvass for his rhetorical style. He spent more than a year tirelessly roaming from town to town, village to village throughout Britain. On his travels O'Connor had discovered a mass movement with an enormous proletarian base. It was already seasoned in the struggle against the New Poor Law and seemed prepared to go beyond constitutional means to achieve its goals if necessary.

The decision to hold a National Convention in London from which the petition would be presented to Parliament brought differences to the fore. The idea of a Convention was rooted in radical tradition running back into the eighteenth century, to Paris in the

1790s and beyond, to revolutionary Philadelphia in the 1770s. But it was an ambiguous concept. Moderates saw it merely as a body to facilitate the presentation of the petition whilst the militants, imbued with Jacobin traditions, saw it as an embryo of an alternative people's parliament.

It is probable that the impact of the Convention was limited by fear of the law of 1799 forbidding assemblies of more than 50 persons. The Convention kept within the restriction[17] but was further hampered by the tentative attitudes of many of its members, especially when the question of physical force was raised. There is also the serious question of just how representative it could be. To leave work, travel from the provinces and sit for months in London, or Birmingham, was beyond the means of working men who formed the enormous mass meetings which elected delegates from many areas. Men of independent means therefore tended to be elected. Consequently only 24 out of the original membership of 53 were in any sense working men. Harassment, arrest and lack of funds took a gradual toll on the delegates. Its inevitable instability given its social composition, its lack of coherence in objectives and the restrictions within which it existed rendered its executive functions weak. This was evident in both the raising of regular funds through a National Rent and the regional patchiness of petitioning.

The assembly sat in London from February to May 1839 when the petition, which had gathered over a million signatures, was ready to be presented. With the economy and Melbourne's government in crisis, there was increasing anxiety at the militant tenor of the radicals and the rash of mass meetings in the provinces. On a resolution of Feargus O'Connor the Convention transferred its business to Birmingham. There militants had snatched the local movement from the hands of the old Political Union leaders who had been largely moderate businessmen. Debates became more militant, calling for a series of 'ulterior measures'. Eight were proposed: withdrawal of funds from savings banks, the conversion of paper money into gold, a sacred month, to defend with arms laws and constitutional privileges, to elect Chartist candidates by a show of hands at the next election and to consider them the people's representatives, to deal exclusively with Chartist trades people, to contend for nothing less than the Charter and to obey all just and constitutional requests of the Convention.

It could be said that this manifesto betrayed the equivocal nature of an assembly under siege. Most points were purely rhetorical. Others, like withdrawal of funds and conversion of currency, were irrelevant to the mass of Chartists who had no property and certainly no bank accounts. Exclusive dealing both left too much to the individual and assumed the presence of very substantial numbers of Chartist-inclined shopkeepers. It did give an important issue for women to organise round. To 'defend with arms' could be taken as rhetoric or as a clear statement of intent.

The 'sacred month' was the one potentially challenging idea. Here, for the first time, was a tactic directly relevant to the mass social base of Chartism in the industrial areas, the proletariat. There has been much debate about its genealogy and meaning.[18] Its architect was William Benbow, a Lancashire working man whose radical history went back to the period before Peterloo. He was a typical ultra-radical and his ideas for both a convention and a 'sacred month' or 'national holiday' (general strike) were not new. Belonging to that political tradition, the ideas were not rooted in economic class analysis but in the political analysis of a people or a nation standing against a parasitic and grasping aristocratic elite and its hangers on. The vision was of a whole people (or virtually so) demonstrating their strength by sheer numbers. The expectation was that this caste would be unlikely to abdicate without a fight and therefore the people should be armed to assert their ultimate superiority. It was anticipated that the hired soldiers, given sight of the masses in arms, would lay down their arms and join their brothers. It was the politics of Paine and Cobbett rather than Robert Owen and the new socialists.

What *was* new was the character of the struggles, reflecting changing social relations, into which these notions were to achieve currency. It was very hard for the new industrial workers to see their managers and employers as fellow sufferers from 'Old Corruption'. Not that there was an immediate transformation. Ideas tend to change in action. Chartist proletarians, no less than artisans and petit bourgeois adherents, went into battle, sometimes literally so, equipped with the strategy and tactics then current. The first severe test was to be in South Wales in November 1839.

The Convention's move to the Midlands had been tracked by the government. A posse of Metropolitan police officers was deployed in Birmingham where a riot took place in the Bull Ring, followed by arrests of Chartists including the militants Peter Murray McDouall and John Collins and the moderate William Lovett. When the issue of the petition was brought before Parliament on 4 July it was summarily dismissed, apparently exposing the critical weakness of the petitioning tactic. The movement was at a point of crisis facing possible disintegration. With the mass platform at least temporarily discredited, militant armed conspiracy was to have its moment.

... the South Wales Rising and its aftermath

Militant Chartism had come to Wales in 1839 but not, initially, to the coalfield areas of the south. In April the Convention had sent a 'missionary', Henry Hetherington, to the depressed linen manufacturing districts of mid-Wales where he had received an encouraging reception. Despite his plea for moral force, the local authorities, fearing that workers were arming, called upon the Home Secretary to send soldiers to protect property. His modest response was to send three Metropolitan police officers. The numbers were token but the symbolism considerable. When the police arrested three local Chartists in the streets of Llanidloes, a crowd rapidly formed. It attacked the hotel where police and prisoners were lodged, freeing the prisoners and attacking the police and the mayor whom they accused of complicity with the authorities.

The leading local Chartist, Thomas Powell, an ironmonger and a moderate, rescued the policemen and the mayor and the riot came to an end. However, the authorities used what was a minor incident to attack the local Chartist leadership which had not been present during the incident and which was largely made up of moral force men. Substantial numbers of troops were brought into the area, warrants were issued and 32 arrests were made. Powell, on entirely trumped-up evidence, was sentenced to twelve months in prison, whilst three Llanidloes men were sentenced to fifteen and seven years transportation for their part in the events. This was the beginning of an attempted crackdown on Chartism in Wales, largely instigated by a nervous yet belligerent local bourgeoisie.

The arrest of Henry Vincent, the 'missionary' who had travelled from the Convention to the West Country, was to have very serious repercussions. Vincent, dubbed 'the tribune of the West', had taken the Chartist message tirelessly up and down the mining and iron-working valleys. He was an orator of immense talent and had spoken in a determinedly militant vein, winning workers to the cause in hundreds. In the early months of 1839 dozens of Chartist cells had been formed, predominantly proletarian, which radically changed the social composition of the movement in Wales. The arrest of Vincent and the harassment of other leading figures in the movement seemed to underline the conclusion that working men and women could expect no favours whatever from the reformed Parliament. Arming and drilling became the order of the day.

When the leaders of the Convention revoked their earlier decision to call a 'sacred month' in August of 1839, opting for a three-day national holiday, the decision was greeted with anger in the valleys and a broad resolve was reached to carry on the militant fight. The catalyst was the pursuit of Chartist leaders and the arrest of some. But the causes of the unrest were rooted in a sharpening class war which had broadened and intensified in the 1830s. Welsh workers had shown fierce resistance to the New Poor Law and had used a terrorist organisation, the Scotch Cattle,[19] active earlier in a strike in 1821, to stop attempts to establish its writ in Wales but also to physically redress all manner of injustices from wage cuts, unwelcome changes in working practices, victimisations, blacklegging, rent increases, evictions and trucking violations. This direct action was highly successful, striking terror into employers, unsympathetic shopkeepers, landlords, magistrates, clerics and workers perceived to be bosses' men. It also appears to have been sanctioned by the communities from which the men hailed, for it was virtually impossible for the law enforcement agencies to catch and expose the cells.

An indigenous police force was almost non-existent in South Wales, and the military was usually holed up in barracks a considerable marching distance, over unsympathetic terrain, from the centres of recently developed industry. The means of inculcating established values were also lacking. Schools hardly existed and perhaps as low as 30 per cent of the population ever darkened a church door.

Industry had come to South Wales, on any scale, within the living memory of the bulk of its participants. Some of the new industrial communities, like Merthyr, were like 'frontier' towns, consisting largely of first and second generation immigrants from England, Ireland and rural Wales. Workers lived in rapidly thrown up accommodation, overcrowded, cold, damp and insanitary. They worked on new industrial sites: coal-mines and iron-works where working conditions were appalling and life for most was brutish and too often short. Subject to crude and violent work discipline and the vagaries of the market, men and women could not even see their wage as their own, since it was too easily forfeited in fines for petty refractions, charges for tools and candles, and the truck (company) shop seen by many workers as the ultimate invasion of citizenship in a generally harsh and uncomfortable existence devoid of amenities.

The mining and iron-working communities had a history of intransigence. Localised rioting, strikes and the actions of the Scotch Cattle created a wary bourgeoisie thinly spread away from the principal administrative and marketing centres like Cardiff, Newport, Abergavenny and Pontypool. Lady Charlotte Guest, wife of the iron founder of Merthyr, remarked that it took courage to live among the miners and iron founders. The arrival of the Chartist missionaries in 1838–39 gave the workers' discontent and anger sharper focus and clearer goals. Inchoate rage was replaced by purposeful organisation, discussion of strategy and a growing and generalised class consciousness. Blackwood colliers argued that 'all other orders are living upon the labour of the so-called lower orders'. Workers at Garndiffaith lodge discussed the take-over of industrial property, 'as the Works do not belong to the present proprietors, but to the Workmen, and they would very shortly have them'.[20] The governing class's wariness was replaced by fear and a strident demand upon the British state for the means to defend property and destroy recalcitrance.

The first Welsh Chartists were petit bourgeois figures, shopkeepers, publicans, attorneys and medical men, disillusioned by the outcome of 1832. Usually moral force in outlook, accustomed to civilised discourse, they were numerically overwhelmed by the enormous influx of the proletariat in 1838–39. Some beat a hasty retreat at the accents of class war, but others adapted, pushed and pulled into leadership roles. This was the position of John Frost, the Newport draper and magistrate, a democrat for at least 20 years by 1839. He declared, 'It is now clear, as the sun at noon day, that the Reform Bill was a humbug, and that it was intended for nothing else.'[21] A delegate to the National Convention, Frost, with such power at his back, sided with the physical force wing. He entered into discussion with those who wished to plan and execute insurrection when petitioning and lobbying were arrogantly rejected by the rulers. Back in Wales, Frost was a front man for a small secret revolutionary leadership of working men. This tiny group, of perhaps three or four, had a confidence borne of the fact that a sizeable network of local leaders developed with astonishing rapidity in the summer and autumn of 1839. It was, in turn, a local leadership carried on a massive tide of popular sentiment. Tens of thousands of working men and women signed the petition for the Charter in those few months. At the peak, in the autumn of 1839, there were over 25,000 paid-up Chartists organised in over 100 lodges, meeting regularly in beer houses and hotels. The spring and summer of 1839 were marked by a series of vast meetings with perhaps over 30,000 at Dukestown on 12 August, the proposed start of the 'sacred month'.

Weeks of careful preparation for insurrection took place before the attack on Newport on 3 November. The leaders roamed the valleys from Tredegar in the west to Pontypool in the east, agitating and recruiting. Almost everywhere the story was of increasing numbers rushing into the new working men's association chapters. The unwilling were pressed into service, though there is evidence that few were inclined to refuse. They were immediately subdivided into cells of eleven with a captain appointed to report to the central body. The evidence suggests that there was a widespread understanding that they were being built into a massive workers' army which would have to fight. Reports of pike-making and drilling with arms were trickling back to the state authorities, though the force did not exist on the ground to check such activity in the localities.[22]

The leaders appeared to have believed they were part of a wider national plan to enforce the Charter on the Parliament by simultaneous risings in several parts of the country, and specifically in Lancashire and West Yorkshire. It appears that such discussions had taken place in October, though communications between areas seem to have been weak. The most voluble of the physical force men, Peter Bussey of Bradford, on his return from the Convention to Yorkshire, seems to have assessed the situation and drawn the conclusion that an insurrection was doomed. Matthew Fletcher of Bury in Lancashire did likewise. Similarly William Ashton of Barnsley drew back from the brink and fled the country. Somehow intelligence of this change of heart did not reach South Wales until after the columns of men had gathered in their local areas and begun to move down the valleys on 2 November.

News of the target of the mass attack was suppressed until the columns of marchers had been tramping through appalling weather for several hours and several thousand were gathered outside Newport. It is not clear whether Frost was suffering a failure of nerve but he certainly delayed the attack, apparently waiting for reinforcements and losing any advantage of surprise by mounting a night-time assault. By the time he did call for a move in the direction of Newport the troops were ensconced in the town.

Another member of the inner councils, John Rees, a veteran of wars in North America, committed a strategic folly by heading directly for the Westgate Hotel where Chartist prisoners taken earlier were being held guarded by soldiers of the 45th Regiment. The incoming workers were easy targets for the soldiers as they lined up outside the hotel. They were mown down by rifle fire. Twenty Chartists were killed and many more injured. The leaders were completely disoriented by their losses, beating a confused retreat pursued by soldiers.

Meanwhile masses of workers were still moving towards Newport. Thousands stood in various villages around the town awaiting orders which never came. There were similar situations in other parts of the coalfield. So great was the groundswell of anger and determination that the will to take on the state's forces was not dissipated for days, but eventually as the army poured into the area the workers were put to flight. They retreated to their home areas in as good order as was possible. Many of the leading local figures were hidden, some escaped to England, the Continent and America, but over 90 were captured as the state sought exemplary revenge for the assault on its privilege.

At the assizes in Newport early in the next year the leaders were brought to trial. John Frost, Zephaniah Williams, William Lloyd Jones and five others were charged with treason and sentenced to death. Two charged with treason escaped and were never tried. The minor leaders and activists were tried for lesser offences. Most were found guilty and served relatively short prison sentences. The local bourgeoisie wanted much harsher treatment because they felt the greater affront through their personal proximity to workers' activity. The national government, however, was anxious to minimise martyrdom. They had the sentences on Frost, Williams and Jones commuted to transportation to Australia; the other five to terms of imprisonment.

The greatest rising of working men and women to date was at an end, but it did not collapse in massive demoralisation. Although South Wales did not feature strongly in the remaining phases of Chartist activity, the 1840s were marked by a growth of trade unionism and a spreading of workers' association. Scotch Cattle activity took a time to die away and the 'Hosts of Rebecca',[23] though largely a rural phenomenon, embraced mining and iron-working communities.

The rising does demonstrate a number of important features of Chartism. It was an enormous mass movement of proletarians. To some extent this feature has been disguised by the smallness of the confrontation in Newport in terms of numbers involved and the brevity of the engagement. Furthermore, the relatively small numbers brought to trial did not mean that only small numbers had been involved, but that there was a remarkable community solidarity protecting those involved from detection. Another remarkable feature, considering there may have been as many as 30,000 men and a few women on the move, was that there were virtually no reports of looting, mindless vandalism, wanton violence or drunkenness. A triumphant and vengeful bourgeois class might have been expected to fully report and inflate such activities, if they had occurred. That they could not do so is an astonishing testimony to the organisation, discipline and purposefulness of those involved.

We know relatively little about the leaders' objectives and this is not perhaps surprising since they would have known that failure, apprehension and trial would have been likely to have meant their deaths. Good sense would demand keeping strategic decisions within a very close band and not committing plans to paper. There is some evidence of an intention to take towns other than Newport. Cardiff, Abergavenny, Brecon and Monmouth (where Vincent was held) have been mentioned. To have mounted a simultaneous assault would appear to have been possible given the numbers known to have been actively marching. Given that the coalfield settlements were by definition in workers' hands and that west Wales would be cut off from the British army, except by sea, a successful operation would have proved a formidable challenge to the state's forces. Furthermore, such an occupation would have been an inspiration to Chartist workers in other parts of Britain. The projected actions in the North might have been revived. In such a situation the government would have had a major problem in restoring its order. If such a plan is implicit in what we know of the intentions of the Welsh leadership, we can perhaps attribute its failure in execution to a combination of factors including strategic indecision on the day, poor communications, unexpectedly long periods of time taken by the marching columns and maybe advanced intelligence of the retreat of would-be English insurgents.

It is possible to view Newport as a complex mixture of past and future strategies. The seizing of power, even on a one town basis, by a determined band owes something to the Jacobin traditions of the radical movement in Britain. Indeed the manual of such activity, by the Italian revolutionary Macerone, was well known in the British movement, having been discussed in the *Northern Star*. Similarly Bronterre O'Brien had translated and published Buonarotti's *Conspiracy of Equals,* the classic left-Jacobin account of the Babeuvist conspiracy in Paris in 1796. It is likely that men like John Frost, Zephaniah Williams and Dr William Price of Pontypridd, one of the best informed of Welsh radicals, would have been familiar with such ideas.

However, the situation in South Wales was somewhat different from Paris in the 1790s. There was a proletarian mass movement conscious and active. There is some evidence that participants were becoming aware of their potential power as the creator of society's wealth. In walking out of the pits and iron-works on 2 November they were displaying that power, but their real strength would have lain in staying out, controlling the local environment, perhaps establishing workers' committees and appealing to workers elsewhere to follow their example. Marching away from base in military-style columns, inadequately armed, to engage in confrontation with trained and disciplined soldiers would almost certainly expose their weakness rather than build on their inherent strength. There is no evidence that discussion of these issues took place in even rudimentary form. Although the venture did not disintegrate immediately upon news of men having fallen at Newport, there is no evidence of any fall-back positions being canvassed or enacted.

As we shall see, however, the movement in 1842 had advanced beyond the thinking of 1839. None of this, though important in our appreciation of the gains and the limitations of Chartism, should detract from our understanding of the events in South Wales as the first generalised insurrectionary activity of the new industrial working class.

If the events of Newport did not massively demoralise the Welsh workers, it did seem to have had that effect elsewhere in Britain. The state power had been especially active since the spring. The most prominent leaders were either in custody or soon would be. They included Feargus O'Connor, Bronterre O'Brien, William Lovett, John Collins, Henry Vincent and Joseph Rayner Stephens. Moreover hundreds of local Chartists found themselves hounded and arrested in the months which followed. There was some revival among the most militant sections of the movement during and after the trial of the men of Newport, and a vast petition calling for the freeing of Frost and his comrades was organised in the spring of 1840.

During the actual trial period in January, activities with an insurrectionary intent took place in Sheffield, Dewsbury, Todmorden, Bradford and Newcastle. None amounted to very much. Such national leaders as were free were certainly not involved. There was probably an organised conspiratorial intent but the news of Newport had limited the circles ready to take part and the Chartists knew of extensive state and local bourgeois preparations to deal with outbreaks. Devyr's account of the situation in Newcastle is interesting. He writes of serious preparations to arm, and of very careful cell organisation, but also of the obvious measures being taken to organise the citizenry with the substantial back-up of troops. Finally, he speaks of his resolve and efforts to restrain his comrades from facing a massacre.[24] Provocateurs were probably active, definitely so in the case of Bradford.[25] So far as can be deduced, in each case relatively small numbers of men were involved in rushing about town and firing weapons. Meaningful targets are not evident and the local authorities had little difficulty in dispersing them and making arrests. In one sense they can be seen tactically as little Newports: poorly armed bands of working men, more or less marching on ill-defined targets. Also, like Newport, the bravery of most was never in question. However, as the first stage of Chartism crumbled into some disarray, it was obvious, at least to some, that the activity of the previous year or so had raised some central questions for the movement.

The National Charter Association

Whilst the Convention had been an umbrella sheltering the many different positions and interests within the movement, its successor was different in conception. The events of 1839–40 had shaken the movement's confidence. Differences had been expressed sharply enough to bring about widespread defection, especially from the middle-class sections of the membership, many of whom found the proposals and activities of Jacobin and proletarian elements unacceptable. Many of the defectors drifted into other campaigns including the Complete Suffrage Union as well as Corn Law

Repeal, educational reform and temperance, but others just dropped out.

The survivors of this first phase of Chartism assessed their weaknesses, concluding that much more efficient organisation was essential. It was in a climate of anxiety that proposals for a more structured national organisation were proffered. The outcome was the National Charter Association (NCA), inaugurated in Manchester in July 1840. Much more bureaucratic than its predecessor, it started with a carefully drawn up 22-point constitution. In some respects it was the first working-class political party in history. The model was a trade union one, drawn from the experience of its substantial working-class membership, with local sections (branches), standard subscription, an elected executive council with paid officials and the responsibility to take decisions.[26]

Whilst the NCA was clearly working-class in its concepts, it prefigures reformist organisational modes rather than revolutionary ones. Such organisation reflected a need to impose policy upon a diverse membership, fissiparous in tendency. Bureaucracy was effected to control the membership whilst it was rationalised in terms of greater efficiency. The problem was that the period demanded both more efficiency to attempt to achieve agreed goals but also a much more flexible organisation, putting the emphasis on the initiative and activity of the membership. 'We must take advantage of every passing event',[27] argued O'Connor, who seems to have understood the requirements better than anyone else, but the NCA fell between two stools. It had a bureaucratic constitution but, except in some areas, a very weak and poorly organised and uncoordinated membership on the ground. Its leadership was quite inadequate in response to the possibilities offered, especially in 1842, when Chartism and militant trade unionism briefly fused in the mass strikes of that year. The most talented leaders with the biggest following, Harney and O'Connor himself, turned their backs on this massive upsurge of working-class activity. After 1842 the organisation limped badly through the 1840s. In several areas its activities atrophied. It was unable to take effective decisions or make the decent ones stick.

CHAPTER 3

The Mass Strike of 1842

The strikes start

> Perhaps the women were at this encounter the more valiant of
> the two; approaching to the very necks of the horses they
> declared they would rather die than starve, and if the soldiers
> were determined to charge they might kill them.[1]

This was August 1842. A reporter was writing from Halifax where
he had witnessed violent street battles between workers and troops.
The town's mills and workshops lay idle. Local workers filled the
streets to welcome columns of strikers marching from Rochdale,
Todmorden, Hebden Bridge to the west and Bradford to the east,
removing plugs from the factory boilers and letting out mill dams
on the way. A young worker, Ben Wilson, remembered that he made
his way to Halifax (from an outlying village),

> as fast as possible, and met them at the top of New Bank. I was
> much surprised when I saw thousands marching in procession,
> many of whom were armed with cudgels ... I then made my way
> to Skircoat Moor, where I had heard there was to be a large
> meeting held, and when I arrived I saw such a sight as I had
> never seen there before, the moor being literally covered with
> men and women.[2]

Workers were on the move. The main action had started in May
in the Black Country where colliers had struck against wage cuts.
By late June it had spread to the Potteries. Some 300 Longton miners
struck to resist a 7d per day wage cut and paraded about the
Potteries seeking support. In early July the Chairman of the Stoke
Board of Guardians warned the Prime Minister, Sir Robert Peel,
that bodies of colliers were patrolling the streets demanding food
or money: 'unless something be done to find employment and
cheaper food ... a struggle will commence, of which no man can
see the extent and consequences'.[3]

A struggle *had* commenced. On 11 July a Central Committee
of Operative Colliers was set up in Hanley and during the following
fortnight colliers throughout the North Staffordshire area were
picketed out. Towards the end of the month the strike seemed to
be crumbling but it got a second wind. In early August the colliers

were out again and so were the potters. Pickets travelled south to Birmingham, West Bromwich and Bilston and the Black Country colliers followed suit, as did those in Shropshire. The struggle was to run on through the summer to September, engaging perhaps half a million workers in the Midlands, Lancashire, Cheshire, Derbyshire, Yorkshire, the Scottish coalfields and Dundee. In these places it took on the character of a general strike.

Supporting actions took place in many other parts of Britain including London, where Charles Darwin was 'incarcerated' in Gower Street:

> For three days, from 14–16 August, battalions of Guards and Royal Horse Artillery marched up through central London to the new Euston Station to put down the riots in Manchester. The troops were trailed by jeering crowds. The commotion was terrible as they passed Darwin's road, with screams of 'Remember, you are brothers,' and 'Don't go and slaughter your starving fellow countrymen.' By the time the battalions reached Gower Street the demonstrators were hemming them in, with gangs everywhere. The streets were frightening, even with a huge police presence. Each day the situation worsened. On the 16th the station (only a few hundred yards from the house) was actually blocked and the troops repeatedly charged the crowds to clear a way in ... For days on end, up to ten thousand demonstrators massed on the commons all over the capital. Working men and women milled about the streets, shouting and cheering.[4]

The depression of 1841–42 had hit the capital hard, stimulating mass support for Chartism. Numerous trades associations affiliated to the National Charter Association in the year of the strike, and more Londoners than anywhere else had signed the second petition to Parliament presented – and rejected – that May.

The epicentre of the strike, however, was the industrial triangle formed by Stalybridge, Ashton and Manchester. Midland colliers were reportedly in the district seeking support, but, for six months, dissent with wage cutting had been bubbling in Lancashire and several brief strikes had taken place, at Hindley in January, at Bolton and Blackburn in March, at Preston in April, and at Stockport and Wigan in July. Chartist Sunday Camp meetings were drawing large crowds through the spring and early summer and industrial action and insurrection were on the agenda.

The catalyst for the eruption of discontent in Lancashire came from Stalybridge at the end of the first week in August. Three firms threatened their weavers with a 25 per cent reduction in wages. One of the masters told his protesting workers 'to go and play for a few days'. That was on Friday 5th. Two days later a mass meeting was held on Mottram Moor, addressed by Chartist speakers. It was agreed to start sending out flying pickets. The Chairman ended the proceedings with this call:

> You people have been told the evils we labour under and I am requested also to tell you that tomorrow a meeting will take place at Stalybridge at five o'clock in the morning, when we will proceed from factory to factory, and all hands that will not willingly come out we will turn them out. And, friends, when we are out, we will remain out, until the Charter which is the only guarantee you have for your wages, becomes the law of the land. I hope to meet you all tomorrow morning at Stalybridge; when we will join hand in hand at this great National turn-out.[5]

During the week which followed thousands of pickets marched through the district turning out an estimated 50,000 workers. The Ashton and Stalybridge strikers saw Manchester as the key to the movement's success and immediate attention was given to overcoming the resistance of the civil and military powers. After two or three days the city's industry was brought to a standstill, led by workers from the large textile and engineering enterprises, some of which had a thousand or more workers. The chief magistrate, Daniel Maude, wrote:

> Number of mills were turned out with such expedition and by such insignificant bodies, as showed that the hands in (I believe) the majority of instances were ready to go out at the first invitation, and rendered it generally impossible for any force to be brought to the required point in time to prevent such a result.[6]

With this area solidly for the strike, attention could be given to the surrounding areas. By the end of the week Stockport[7] and Macclesfield to the south had followed and to the north most of Oldham, Bolton, Rochdale, Preston and Bury. During the second week Eccles and Blackburn struck and the movement crossed the Pennines bringing Todmorden, Hebden Bridge, Halifax, Dewsbury and much of Bradford to a standstill. The method of spreading the action was broadly the same everywhere: mass rolling picketing.

The strikers would assemble in the early morning in thousands to hear militant speeches: 3000 in Stalybridge, 14,000 in Ashton Market Place, 10,000 in Oldham on 8 August, up to 20,000 in Ashton, 20,000 on Granby Row Fields, Manchester on the 9th and 15,000 in the same place on the following day; 'several thousand' in Bolton also on the 10th, and 30,000 on Cronky Field, Rochdale on the 11th. The meetings would then divide into 'smaller' parties which would march off to the smaller towns and villages, turning out en route and accumulating fresh pickets. By mid-August half a million workers had joined the action.

Background

On 1 January 1842, the *Northern Star* published an item entitled 'The State of the Country' which started sardonically with a quotation from the Duke of Wellington. It ran, 'This is the only country in the world in which every labouring man can by industry obtain a competency.' There followed reports on workers' conditions from several northern and Scottish towns. The most striking was from Bradford which included some 20 extracts from case notes made by visitors to workers' homes that winter. One read:

> A woolcomber from Ireland, out of work seven weeks – has four children, the eldest eight years – has travelled in search of work in vain. They have not a penny to depend on. Their furniture was sold up a fortnight since. An old black sheet and a little straw formed their bed; have applied twice unsuccessfully to the overseers unless they would return to Ireland, where they supposed they would be no better off. The mother would die in the house rather than beg.

The reporter commented that such a case was:

> a fair sample of two thirds of working families in Bradford, reduced not by sickness, but by inadequate employment. In several cases of sickness the medical gentlemen called in have said it was not physic but food that was required. One half of the working men of Bradford appear to be sinking under poverty or exhaustion. One sixth of operative families of Bradford are unemployed, two thirds are suffering from deficient employment. Not above a third are in full work.[8]

The year of 1842 was probably the bleakest for working people since the coming of an industrial society. The samples quoted above from Bradford were part of a common pattern of political reports from the towns of Britain which were regularly featured in the the *Northern Star* that year. If anything, though, much more stark were the news columns, where, mixed with stories of murders, robberies, and train derailments, there were two or three stories per issue of people dying from starvation.

Unemployment and short-time working struck at every industry and every area of Britain. Falling demand hit hardest of all at the handloom weavers, woolcombers, and other groups of outworkers, already suffering long-term distress from competition with the new factory sector. Weavers' wages had fallen by some 80 per cent over two decades and by the 1840s the surviving branches had been marginalised and their workers reduced to desperation.

The Factory Inspectors reported in spring 1842 that 78 per cent of workers in Leigh were unemployed or on short time, 58 per cent in Wigan, 50 per cent in Bolton, 48 per cent in Ashton, and that a group of large firms in Manchester previously employing 15 per cent of the labour force had ceased trading. A similar picture was reported from Paisley in Scotland, much of West Yorkshire and the West Midlands.

The employers' method of dealing with the erosion of their profit margins was to make the workers pay – by cutting wages. In this period wages were invariably fixed at around subsistence level and therefore any cut could spell disaster for the working-class family. At his trial at Lancaster in 1843, Richard Pilling, an outstanding working-class strike leader, put before the court his personal history. In respect of wage cutting he said that in the past few years (before the strike) he had suffered seven separate pay cuts. Of one, he said:

> the master manufacturers ... gave us notice for a reduction of one penny a cut. Some people think a penny is a small reduction, but it amounts to five weeks wages in the course of the year. It is 2s. 6d. a week ... they were robbing every operative of five weeks wages.[9]

The consequences of such cuts were dire. Pilling went on to record that his earning had been brought down to something like sixteen shillings a week when rent cost three shillings, 'one shilling and sixpence for fire, sixpence for soap and two shillings for clothing'. Sixteen shillings 'is all I had to live on, with my nine in family ... and a sick son lying helpless before me. I have gone home and seen that son [here Pilling was moved to tears, and unable to proceed for some time] I have seen that son lying on a sick bed and dying pillow, and having nothing to eat but potatoes and salt.'[10]

Wage cutting was general throughout the depression and had hit workers in most industries and every region. It was certainly the single most important issue behind the strike. Specifically, the action of Midlands mine owners in May and Stalybridge factory masters in August drove the workers over the edge and into action.

However, the explosion of that summer should also be seen as a culmination of at least two decades of workers' frustration and rage with the rapidly changing system in which they were trapped. These included the exactions of the new factory system, the increasing pressures of small workshop labour, the failure effectively to reduce working hours, the appalling living conditions in the 'new' industrial areas and the terror associated with the implementation of the New Poor Law.

Almost anything was preferable to facing the Poor Law Guardians. In May, the *Northern Star* reported workhouses in a number of towns being protected by the military. In Stockport in August unemployment had reached 75 per cent. The 'new bastille' was raided and looted by workers seeking bread.

There is one final piece of the strike's backcloth to consider: Chartist activity in the pre-strike period. Much of the spring of the year had been taken up in gathering signatures for a further petition of Parliament. This was drawn up by the Convention of the National Charter Association which met in April. The petition was colossal, amounting to over three million signatures and is a testament to the widespread network of organisation the Chartists had built up in the previous year. It was overwhelmingly rejected by the House of Commons in early May. A leading opponent was Lord Macauley, who said:

> I believe that universal suffrage would be fatal to all purposes for which government exists, and for which aristocracies and all other things exist, and that it is utterly incompatible with the very existence of civilisation. I conceive that civilisation rests on the security of property ... If I understand this petition rightly, I believe it to contain a declaration, that the remedies for the evils of which it complains ... are to be found in a great and sweeping confiscation of property ... I will oppose with every faculty which I possess the proposition for universal suffrage.[11]

In its issue following rejection the *Northern Star* stated:

> Three and a half millions have quietly, orderly, soberly, peaceably, but firmly asked of their rulers to do justice; and their rulers have turned a deaf ear to that protest. Three and a half millions of people have asked permission to detail their wrongs, and enforce their claims for RIGHT, and the 'House' has resolved they should not be heard! Three and a half millions of the slave-class have holden out the olive branch of peace to the enfranchised and privileged classes and sought for a firm and compact union, on the principal of EQUALITY BEFORE THE LAW; and enfranchised and privileged have refused to enter into a treaty! The same class is to be a slave class still. The mark and brand of inferiority is not to be removed. The assumption of inferiority is still to be maintained. The people are not to be free.[12]

With repeated wage cuts and a further insulting denial of political manhood to working people, the stage was set for conflict that summer.

Building the strike

The day-by-day progress of the strike appears to have been achieved by simple instructions, at enormous open air meetings, followed by marching columns of workers dispersing over the countryside turning out other workers. There was a tradition of such activity in Lancashire running back at least to the great strikes of 1818.[13]

The tactic had been employed in the area in 1839. The Chartists in many districts were clearly confused and demoralised by the abrupt change in tactics over the 'sacred month'. However, in the cotton districts north and west of Manchester (Bolton, Bury, Heywood, Middleton, Leigh) mass mobile picketing achieved virtual solidarity for the three-day strike.[14]

Workers in the Manchester area also had experience of delegate conferences going back at least two decades. Conferences drawing together trades from different areas and cross-trades conferences had been held on many issues, such as the strikes of 1810[15] and 1818, opposition to the New Poor Law, support for a reduction in the working day, defence of the Dorchester Labourers and the Glasgow Cotton Spinners, and, most recently, promotion of Corn Law repeal. In March 1842 such a meeting went desperately wrong for the Anti-Corn Law advocates when a large majority of delegates substituted agitation for the People's Charter for repeal of the Corn Laws. Working men were apparently simultaneously separating themselves from a middle-class cause and submerging their sectionalism in a drive for a *class* political solution. It was no isolated event, for in the spring and summer meetings of cordwainers, shoemakers, fustian cutters, and joiners declared for the Charter and affiliated to the National Charter Association. In mid-July a meeting of hammermen in Manchester received deputations from mechanics and smiths and informed them:

> that their trades, after maturely examining the subject, had found that the trades' unions had not accomplished that for which they had been formed, namely the protection of the labour of the working man; and, therefore, they had come to the conclusion that nothing short of a participation in the making of laws by which they were governed, would effectively protect their labour. Having come to that conclusion they had joined the National Charter Association.[16]

The affiliation of the engineering trades was very significant. They were numerous among skilled workers and strategically placed in workshops which were the largest apart from textiles. Relatively privileged among workmen, many of them had previously tended to stay aloof from political movements and even from any cross-trade co-operation. The depression, with its wage cutting, short time and an acceleration of technical change which hit engineers especially hard, clearly threatened their status, producing the impetus to seek political solutions.

This was the background to the series of delegate conferences held in Manchester from the start of the strike's second week. On

12 August a meeting was held of trades' delegates and mill hands. This was attended by over 200 delegates from a very wide range of trades. They reported on the situation in their trade and declared:

> That the only remedy for the present alarming distress and widespread destitution is the immediate and unmutilated adoption and carrying into law [with] the document known as the People's Charter. That this meeting recommends the people of all trades and calling forthwith to cease work until the above document becomes the law of the land.[17]

On the 15th a further general trades conference was held for delegates from Manchester and beyond that immediate area. Some 85 trades gave delegate reports, the great majority being for the Charter. Only a few trades were unrepresented: from 'the most secure artisan trades' such as coachbuilders, printers and bookbinders. There were 55 delegates from some 16 towns or villages beyond Manchester to add to 89 from the city. On its second day the meeting was broken up by the authorities. This was probably the most representative meeting of the whole crisis.

Many accounts of Chartism see Chartists and trade unionists as separate entities. The evidence of the mass strike is of an extremely close correspondence between the two. Furthermore, the strike has usually been depicted as a spontaneous upsurge of starving operatives, incandescent for a brief moment, then falling leaderless into obscurity. In short, it is argued, the economic and political struggles were quite separate and the evidence of Chartist demands being made by strikers derived from opportunism by some Chartist activists. What is more, such demands tended to fade quite rapidly.

In spite of the ambivalent and even plainly hostile attitudes to the strike of some of the main national leaders of the Chartist movement, it is clear that the strike leadership was in the hands of dedicated Chartists who were also, in the main, striking industrial workers themselves. Most of the speakers and organisers in both Lancashire and the Potteries, who were indicted at Lancaster and Stafford Assizes in the wake of the strike or who were listed in the *Northern Star,* were Chartists *and* trade unionists. A number of them had been active in their areas long before the summer of 1842 and some had attended the National Charter Association Conference in the previous year.

Further support for a view of the impact of Chartism in the working class before the strike is lent by a poll reported in August 1842 by the *Dundee Warder* on the question of a possible strike. Of the town's 51 textile mills, 46 were represented at a meeting to discuss strike action. Of those who said they would strike, the overwhelming majority (37) said they would strike for the Charter rather than simply economic demands. The historian Dorothy

Thompson writes: 'Clearly the Dundee workmen, like the more desperate Lancashire operatives, did not consider that their problems – of wages or of political status – could be dealt with by deals with individual employers.'[18]

Richard Otley, an indicted worker, perhaps summed the situation up best, in his trial at Lancaster:

> Great labour has been expended in endeavouring to trace the turn out for wages to us (the Chartists); but, gentlemen, take this into consideration, that in the manufacturing districts there are, at least, four out of every five of the working classes, that either are actually Chartists, or hold Chartist principles. This being the case, it is quite impossible that there should be a turn out for wages, without having a great number of Chartists among the turn outs.[19]

Among the most prominent worker leaders were Richard Pilling and Alexander Hutchison. Pilling, aged 43, was a powerloom weaver working in the town of Ashton at the time of the strike. A former handloom weaver, present at Peterloo, he had been active throughout the 1830s in the Reform Bill agitation, the Ten Hours Movement, and the campaign to free the Glasgow Cotton Spinners. He was arrested, but released in 1839 at the height of the first Chartist upsurge. From 1840 he was central to the Stockport area agitation against wage cuts and in the spring of 1842 a leader of that activity in Ashton and Stalybridge. He chaired mass meetings as the strike took off and led columns of strikers in turning out other factories in the whole of south Lancashire. He was arrested in Ashton on 12 September, trying to hold the line against a then crumbling strike. He was tried at Lancaster in the following spring on charges of sedition, conspiracy, tumult and riot. He defended himself in a speech which can be seen as a biography of the new factory proletariat coming to the painful realisation that mass action was essential if workers were ever to gain power. After explaining his life's struggle for subsistence wages to support his wife and family he ended: 'And, now, Gentlemen of the jury, you have the case before you; the masters conspired to kill me, and I combined to keep myself alive.'[20]

From the tradition of craft trade union organisation came Alexander Hutchinson. At 35, he was a skilled smith and an Owenite socialist active in the Grand National Consolidated Trades Union in the early 1830s. At the time of the strike he was working at the world's largest machine manufacturer, Sharp, Roberts and Co. of Manchester, and held the positions of lay general secretary of the smiths' trade union and editor of the *Trades Journal* which advocated unity across all metal trades. He wrote:

You are all engaged upon the same work – often in the very same workshops; your interests are inseparably the same. Yet when an oppression comes, your employers do not reduce you all at one time; it better serves their end to do it gradually, and when one or two branches have been conquered the rest become an easy prey ... Instead of one shop or place having little disturbances, let it be general, and by such a practice we shall avoid that ill-feeling and contention I have before mentioned.[21]

Hutchinson was also a Chartist. He had led his society on a great demonstration through Manchester in October 1838. He took the chair at a meeting called in March 1842 to organise a mass demonstration in support of the Charter on Kersal Moor where he had stated: 'That his trade would come out for the Charter and nothing else.'[22] He was the chair at the general trades conference on 16 August. At the start of proceedings he stated:

[I have] seen a great change in the opinion of the working men of Manchester ... They were as earnest as ever and appeared to see more than ever the necessity of a great struggle for their political rights ... They would not be men if they did not adopt every measure they could to ensure a triumph and gain their political rights.[23]

He was arrested and charged shortly after the conference was broken up by the authorities.

Pilling and Hutchinson were two of the better known worker leaders of the strike. Many more have been identified from the columns of the *Northern Star,* the *Manchester Guardian* and the trials which followed the strike's end – in the Midlands, Yorkshire and Scotland, as well as the 'storm centre' in Lancashire.

Many of these less prominent figures had long histories of political and trade union activity. John Richards, Convention delegate and Stoke shoemaker, arrested and gaoled in his seventies, had been active for 30 years and Joseph Capper, the Tunstall blacksmith, some 20 years. Thomas Mayer and George Hemmings, Hanley colliers, had been committed Chartists, at least, in the months prior to the strike.

So there was unquestionably a close relationship in 1842 between Chartism and the mass strike. The key local leaders, who are known to us, were all Chartists with a history of radical political activity. The balance of evidence is that the shaping of demands and the planning and leading of initiatives were undertaken by Chartist strikers of some standing and experience in the workers' movement. Given the apparent levels of organisation, the relationship between trades conferences and mass meetings, mass meetings and turn-outs, economic and political demands, the rapid spread of the strike, the solidarity actions beyond the key areas, and the discipline and order of the strikers, it would be remarkable if there had not been an experienced leadership rooted in the working-class communities.

When set against some of the obstacles faced, the scale and intensity of the strike is astonishing. For instance, the nationally known leaders of the Chartist movement were split with a majority openly hostile, others only lukewarm in their support and only a few recognising the transforming capacities of a successful mass strike. Bronterre O'Brien had been firmly against the 'sacred month' in 1839 on the grounds that the movement was not prepared for it. In 1842, recently out of prison, he was in the throes of a violent quarrel with O'Connor over attitudes to support for the middle-class Complete Suffrage Union. He was struggling to hold together his new paper, the *British Statesman,* and 'kept clear of the meetings, strikes and riots which swept through the midlands and the north'.[24] Julian Harney had been the leading advocate of the 'national holiday' or general strike in 1839. He believed that such a strike would signal a national insurrection. At the Manchester Convention of the NCA on 17 August he spoke out strongly against a national strike, believing that insufficient preparation doomed it to disaster. Four days later in Sheffield where he was Chartist organiser he asked a mass meeting: 'Are you ready to fight the soldiers?' He went on:

> You may say that this is not the question but I tell you that it would be the question. I do not think you are. I am ready to share your perils but I will not lead you against the soldiers.[25]

Feargus O'Connor equivocated. Attending the Manchester meeting having opposed support for the strike, he said that he had no enthusiasm for it but voted in favour since it seemed to reflect the will of the majority. He left the Convention for London saying nothing further but subsequently repeating his charge that the strike had been fomented by Anti-Corn Law League factory masters.

Three prominent national figures gave whole-hearted support to the strike. They were Peter Murray McDouall, Thomas Cooper and James Leach. McDouall came from the first phase of Chartism in 1838–40 with a much clearer view of how progress could be achieved. He saw the working class as the only force which could bring about Chartist objectives. This meant working through the unions where possible and building local occupational Chartist associations amongst workers where unions were weak. The strike was a key weapon. In 1841–42 he trudged around the industrial areas of northern Britain speaking at dozens of meetings including vast assemblies in Glasgow of over 100,000 and little ones of a handful in farmyard barns. Some sense of his style comes across from a piece in the *Northern Star:*

> I lectured in a barn where there were two pigs outside and two policemen inside. The pigs grunted, the policemen grumbled and the people were gratified. The policemen were sent for by an old lady who either imagined we were going to storm the house or steal the pigs. The pigs remained unmolested to digest the first Chartist lecturer ever to address the swinish multitude ...[26]

Especially active in south-east Lancashire, he was a central figure in the formation of the National Charter Association in 1841, emphasising the need to build in the localities from the bottom.[27] At the NCA meeting in Manchester on 17 August it was McDouall who put the motion calling for all-out support for the strikers. It was the natural outcome of the work he had done over the past two years.

Thomas Cooper likewise was fully committed. On 9 August he had set out on foot from Leicester to Staffordshire. He spoke to a meeting of 30,000 striking colliers in Wednesbury, doing further meetings at Bilston, Wolverhampton and Stafford. He arrived in Hanley on the 15th chairing a meeting of 8–10,000 colliers and potters where the resolution was put and passed: 'That all labour cease until the People's Charter becomes the law of the land.'[28] He then travelled north to Manchester for the NCA meeting, noting that in 'the City of Long Chimneys ... every chimney was beheld smokeless'.[29] At the conference he followed McDouall in counselling support for the strike:

> I would vote for the resolution because it meant fighting and I saw it must come to that. The spread of the strike would and must be followed by a general outbreak. The authorities of the land would try to quell it; but we must resist them. There was nothing now but a physical force struggle to be looked for. We must get the people out to fight; and they must be irresistible, if they were united.[30]

Like Pilling and Hutchinson, James Leach of Manchester was a working man. A former weaver turned bookseller, he had been an active Chartist since 1838. He was elected to the Executive Committee of the NCA in 1841. He had been in the forefront of the Lancashire strike movement throughout the summer and had travelled widely, promoting Chartism and seeking support for the strike. He was perhaps the best known Chartist lecturer in the Lancashire area and had devoted much time to visiting trades' meetings to solicit support for the Charter. His appeal to workers is evident from the clear class character of his analysis in his defence at his trial at Lancaster in 1843:

Is it not a truth, that, while the warehouses of Manchester are at this moment ready to break down with the superabundant weight of the goods piled in them, the result of the slavery and toil of the industrious classes of England, those who have produced the cloth have not, themselves, a decent suit of clothes to put on their backs ...[31]

Within a week of the meeting of 17 August he was arrested, as was Thomas Cooper, then back in Leicester. McDouall was on the run. He escaped to exile in France.

Clearly there was a serious problem with the leadership of the strike movement. In the districts, leadership of the day-to-day, indeed hour-to-hour, activity was largely in the hands of proletarian Chartists. Their activity suggests that they clearly understood the need to spread the strike rapidly and to give it political direction. Within their areas they were remarkably successful. However, they confronted enormous problems. Apart from the formidable power of the state, they were trying to lead hundreds of thousands of workers who had virtually no resources to live on, in a society where almost the only means of workers communicating from place to place was on foot. The factory workers in one town or village turned out by mass pickets on one day were exposed to the intimidation or modest blandishments of their employers on the next, when the mass pickets had passed on. The strikes which appear to have spread like a tidal wave in the first two weeks or so, required dramatic news of ongoing defiance from other industrial areas and the capital to sustain solidarity. After the strike's second week, this news was not forthcoming.

The movement needed a coherent national leadership travelling and agitating through meetings, newspapers and pamphlets. McDouall, Cooper and a few others tried very hard but they were working alone without the authority or direction of the leadership. No meeting of the NCA took place between April, when the second petition was presented to Parliament, and 17 August, when the strike was already two weeks old. Although the Manchester Convention voted overwhelmingly to support and promote the strike, some of the ablest leaders were either hostile or equivocal. No agitational pamphlets were produced and the *Northern Star*, whilst reporting events, gave no advice to its readers. In fact, the editor, William Hill, was actually the leading opponent of the strike resolution at Manchester.

An overall strategy was also necessary. There was profound hostility to the rulers. There was also a sense that the achievement of the Charter was the route to change. The most positive of the leaders seem to have thought in terms of insurrection but it is not apparent how they believed it would be achieved, beyond the rather vague notion that revolutionary enthusiasm would carry the day. No evidence exists of leaders whose thinking on the general strike went much further than that of William Benbow. Neither workplace organisation nor trade unionism featured much in his project. It does appear that McDouall had some sense of the need for workplace preparation for he argued for linking trade unionism and Chartism and for the formation of Chartist organisation among workers where trade unionism was weak or non-existent. Benbow himself was still active in 1842, among the London shoemakers, but does not seem to have been particularly influential among London Chartists at that time.

Inadequate leadership employing vague and indeterminate strategies was certainly an important factor in determining both the incidence and the destiny of the strike. So, too, of course was the power of the state. Before turning to that it is worth considering if there is anything to be learnt from the character of the industrial structure in the 1840s.

It would be tempting to see the ultimate crumbling of the strike simply in terms of the superior power of the state – once it had regained its footing. There may be some sense in this. After all the British army was a force armed, drilled and fed to destroy antagonists in many different parts of the world. The workers had few arms beyond cudgels, sticks and stones. They had no experience in dealing with set-piece confrontations. But there is another side to the story.

The Midland strikers closed down the potteries, coal pits and forges of the Potteries and the Black Country, but they never penetrated Birmingham, the biggest industrial city. In Yorkshire, although the industrial villages around Leeds were brought to a standstill, no effective bridgehead to the city was established. Despite parades and meetings, the turn-outs in Sheffield were few and short-lived. Apparently industrial Tyneside and the coalfields of Durham were relatively untouched by the strike movement. South Wales, still wounded from the carnage of Newport only three years previously, was relatively passive, and the Rebecca Riots did not peak until the autumn when the main strike wave elsewhere was over.

The known connections are few between the strike in England and the turn-outs in the Scottish coalfields and the textile mills of Dundee. In the case of Dundee, at least, the height of activity appears to have been in the latter part of August when the English movement was already in decline. There is no sign of substantial activity in the textile areas of the Clyde basin. Finally, the capital had a series of large demonstrations. There is evidence of much anger and harassment of troops heading for the North, but there is no evidence of a major strike movement.

So, there was a situation of immense unevenness. It is not accidental that the real manifested power of the working class was in south-east Lancashire. An acute contemporary observer, William Cooke Taylor, travelled through Lancashire's manufacturing districts in the summer of 1842. He wrote:

> As a stranger passes through the masses of human beings which have been accumulated round mills and print works ... he cannot contemplate these 'crowded hives' without feelings of anxiety and apprehension almost amounting to dismay. The population, like the system to which it belongs, is NEW; but it is hourly increasing in breadth and strength. It is an aggregate of masses, our conceptions of which clothe themselves in terms that express something portentous and fearful. We speak not of them indeed as of sudden convulsions, tempestuous seas, or furious hurricanes, but as of the slow rising and gradual swelling of an ocean which must, at some future and no distant time, bear all the elements of society aloft upon its bosom, and float them – Heaven knows where. There are mighty energies slumbering in those masses.[32]

Taylor was to see not only this latent power, but also the strike in progress. He several times draws attention to the disciplined conduct of the strikers in relation to property. Several writers have pointed, especially in the Lancashire context, to workers drawing plugs or emptying boilers but doing no further damage to the workshops. Taylor was also impressed that hordes of hungry strikers passed by an unguarded cherry tree in a factory master's garden without touching a fruit. In the Potteries the strikers were not nearly so restrained. There were several destructive rampages at the peak of the strike, but even here, examination shows selectivity in targets: especially unpopular bosses, managers and magistrates. Taylor and other commentators have also remarked upon the few incidences of theft reported during the strike – with the exception of the taking of bread. Even hostile witnesses at the big Lancaster trial conceded such points. Such discipline seems to have been internalised, although 'stewards' among pickets were sometimes reported to have restrained others. Another feature of the strike in Lancashire commented upon was the establishment of 'Committees of Public Safety' which dealt with employers' appeals for exemption from the strike. All such examples of what might be called 'workers' order' seem to emanate from a sense of power deriving from the

workers' status as part of large workforces, where collective action
appeared to be the only rational means of achieving goals.

Contemporaries, like Cooke Taylor, were quite clear in their
understanding that factories and factory districts represented a
new social phenomena. The Frenchman, Alexis de Tocqueville,
visiting Manchester in 1835 vividly depicts the 'new order':

> An undulating plain, or rather a collection of little hills. Below
> the hills a narrow river ... the Irwell, which flows slowly to the
> Irish sea. Two streams ... the Meddlock and the Irk ... wind
> through the undulating ground and after a thousand bends, flow
> into the river. Three canals made by man unite their tranquil
> lazy waters at the same point. On this watery land, which nature
> and art have contributed to keep damp, are scattered palaces
> and hovels ... *Thirty or forty factories rise on top of the hills I have
> just described. Their six stories tower up; their huge enclosures give
> notice from afar of the centralisation of industry.*[33] (my emphasis)

The rapid technological growth of the cotton industry had also
produced a cluster of engine and machine manufacturers in the area.
The largest in 1841 were Hibbert and Platt in Oldham with 900,
Sharp and Roberts, Manchester with 800 and Nasmyth's
Bridgewater foundry at Patricroft with 300–500.[34] George Nasmyth
was a special constable in 1842 and we know, from his evidence
at the Lancaster trial, that his workers were deeply involved in the
strike.[35]

By the standards of the late nineteenth and twentieth centuries,
cotton and engineering factories were not large, but they did
represent a qualitative change in the experience of both working
people and their rulers. They produced large concentrations of
workers in individual factories and in factory districts. There were
over 70 such places in Manchester alone. Their size demanded an
intensification of supervision and strict discipline. The gap was
widened between workers and bosses.

Altogether this gave the factory districts of south-east Lancashire
a weight not experienced elsewhere in 1842. Turning out two or
three big factories or mills in a small geographical area could
immediately augment the flying pickets by several hundred. It is
easy to see what the impact on dozens of smaller adjacent workshops
might have been. Whilst problems of organisation were formidable,
it would also be relatively easy to monitor the mood of strikers and
to hold the strike together after the turn-out.

By the 1840s every industrial area had a number of large
workshops but only south-east Lancashire had concentrations of
them. Although large workshops might have been prominent in
starting the action in other areas, they could be isolated from each

other by distance. Pulling out lots of little shops would be corre-spondingly more difficult, as would holding the line later. This may have been a problem in West Yorkshire where we have a much more sporadic impression of the strike's impact. The woollen and worsted industries were still very varied in their organisation. Although factories undertaking spinning and weaving were rapidly emerging, many processes were still firmly located in tiny village workshops and homes. The new factories themselves were much smaller on average than those in cotton and, with the exception of Bradford which had perhaps 20 firms with over 100 workers, most were in isolated, or relatively isolated, situations.

Leeds was a town with few large mills and many very small shops especially in the surrounding villages. Apparently the strike came late to Leeds and was of very short duration. This factor might also have been an element in the failure to carry Birmingham for the strike. The Potteries did have some sizeable concerns with over 500 workers but the workforce was usually spread over very large sites, or several sites working in small specialised parts of the process.

Although the size of the large workshop sector might be an important factor in understanding what made Lancashire different, it does not of course explain the extraordinary response to the strike in some other areas where large workshops did not prevail. In the Black Country, Staffordshire, Shropshire and central Scotland, colliers, almost all from tiny pits, formed the backbone of the strike and were among its most militant adherents. Working in a large place may have given to strikers an added sense of their collective power, but not doing so did not preclude strong class identity and behaviour. The majority of workers in Britain of the 1840s had long been subjected to a subordinate relationship borne of capitalism's accumulation process. In work they faced long hours, low wages, dreadful environments and deskilling. Outside of work they experienced overcrowding in insanitary accommodation. Out of work they faced the new workhouses. Their lack of citizenship had been underscored by the outcome of the 1832 Reform Act, and more recently by the House of Commons rejecting the Chartist petition on 3 May.

The highly skilled could expect to do a little better than the displaced or the mass of labourers, but all were subject to great insecurity during the depression which had stuttered on through the late 1830s and into the 'hungry' 1840s. Wage cutters did not distinguish between workers in large and small workshops. Resistance to wage cuts and the appeal of the People's Charter may have been a catalyst for the release of a lifetime's anguish and could affect workers from many different situations. On the other hand, perhaps,

tenacity, discipline and organisational aptitudes might be expected
to come most readily in the factory sector.

The end of the strike and its aftermath

The momentum of the strikes appears to have been halted
towards the end of the second week. A massive flying picket in
Burslem was dispersed on 16 August by a troop of dragoons and
special constables and over 200 workers were arrested over the
following days. Notwithstanding the attack on the soldiers at Salter
Hebble on the 16th, a carriage full of prisoners was transported to
Wakefield Gaol. Turn-outs were still taking place in Bradford
district on the 17th. Keighley mills had been closed by 8000 pickets
from outside that town. However, the centre of Bradford was
occupied by the Lancers and large numbers of prisoners were
taken. A week of desultory attacks from pickets followed with
many arrests and the despatch of 60 prisoners to York Castle.

In the Leeds villages the turn-outs began only on the 17th,
following a Hunslet meeting of 4000 workers declaring for the
Charter the previous evening. Leeds district mills were almost
solid and several pits were closed. Just south of the river, in Holbeck,
massed pickets were attacked by the Lancers under Prince George
and dispersed. Some 38 strikers were arrested; 14 more were taken
at the collieries on Friday and 1000 infantrymen entered the town.
A drift back to work followed.

As early as the 14th troops had fired on and killed four workers
in Preston. The Home Secretary, Sir James Graham, congratulated
the Mayor on his courage. Graham was the resolute organiser of
the forces of the state. He had the foresight to see the importance
of the trades conference and gave orders for its delegates to be
arrested: 'It is quite clear that these Delegates are the directing body;
they form the link between the Trade Unions and the Chartists,
and a blow struck at this Confederacy goes to the heart of the evil
and cuts off its ramifications.'[36] Graham sent a Metropolitan
magistrate to Manchester to stiffen the resolve of the local authorities.
The conference was broken up and five delegates were arrested,
though the rump continued to meet for a week. By the time of these
arrests the NCA conference was in session. It too was broken up
by the troops and in all 60 delegates were arrested.

Meanwhile more and more troops were pouring into the North,
including a regiment withdrawn from Ireland, 500 Grenadier
Guards, 36 Royal Horse Artillerymen and their field pieces sent
by rail from London. All were barracked in the centre of Manchester.

Mounted special constables were used for communications and the pensioners organised in divisions of 20 for street patrol.

Not surprisingly the strike in Manchester began to crumble. After a week of the authorities' harassment, only the powerloom weavers stayed out. They did not return until the 26 September. Outside of the town the strikers were also under severe pressure from hunger, summary arrest and the bribery of employers who conceded the demand for no pay cuts, though Ashton, Stalybridge, Hyde and a number of villages around south-east Lancashire held out until mid-September.

Once organised, the state had enough power to deal with the strike and prevent escalation into insurrection. As we have seen, however, the conflict was not entirely one-sided. Had just two or three other areas, like Tyneside, Sheffield or South Wales, joined the strike, the resources of the state would have been seriously stretched. It was fortunate for the government that it could concentrate its main military resources in just Manchester, Leeds, Newcastle under Lyme, the Lothians and London.

The largest and most militant strike of the century was effectively over by the end of August. What remained was the vengeance of the state. Over 1500 workers were arrested throughout Britain. Of these, 800 were tried by magistrates and 700 were brought before Special Commissions. At Stafford 276 people were tried: 49 were transported and 116 imprisoned. The Cheshire Commission tried 66 strikers variously with riot, conspiracy, felony, and sedition. Four were transported for life, one to 15 years, transportation, five to ten years, transportation, and three to seven years, transportation. Six received two years' imprisonment, five 18 months and one 16 months. The Liverpool Commission sentenced eleven men to transportation and imprisoned 115. Similarly savage sentences were meted out at further Special Commissions.[37]

> The chief judge was Lord Abinger. He spoke for his class when he said: The doctrines promulgated by the chartists were doctrines of perfect insanity, and no man but a fool or a knave could promulgate them ... the establishment of the charter would become an odious tyranny ... They [the executive committee of the NCA] ... wanted to carry the principal of the charter ... that is to say the labouring classes who have no property are to make laws for those who have property.[38]

The workers were to be taught a lesson in class power and political economy. The idea that riot and industrial action could alter the laws of the market were absurd and must be hammered home for the 'industrious classes, who, [have not] competent

minds or sufficient knowledge to form a judgement of their own ...'.[39]
This was the meaning of the harsh sentences passed upon hundreds
of workers in the immediate aftermath of the strike.

The leaders of the NCA apprehended after the Manchester
conference were much more fortunate. Their trials were postponed
until the following spring at Lancaster, apparently with the intention
of preparing a case which would have condemned them to life
imprisonment. Shortly after the autumn trials there were members
of the ruling class severely questioning what Mick Jenkins calls 'the
Peterloo touch' of the judiciary. A critical motion received over 60
votes in the House of Commons. Further savagery might harden
opposition to a government in some difficulty. The depression
showed no signs of amelioration and Prime Minister Peel was
facing the rupture of his party coalition over the Corn Laws.
Certainly in court the prosecuting council and the judge, whilst
condemning the actions of the strikers, implied that the intensity
of the recession had given working people some cause to complain.
The defendants were convicted at Lancaster but, on a legal
technicality, freed without sentence.

It is still not entirely clear why the authorities softened their
approach, but Jenkins makes out a convincing case that there was
a conscious move to hint at the possibility of conciliation as one
remedy to the fierce and powerful hatred that was increasingly
characterising class relations in this period.[40]

The 1842 mass strike was an important landmark in working-
class history. Engels took the view that it marked 'the decisive
separation of the proletariat from the bourgeoisie'. Certainly the
refusal of the workers to accept the guidance of the Anti-Corn Law
League at a moment of maximum desperation was significant.
Engels was probably wrong in arguing that the Anti-Corn Law
manufacturers manoeuvred the workers into strike action, but it
probably did help to give some of them a breathing space when
lay-offs were an alternative. However, there is no doubting their
shock at the intensity of the hostility shown to them by the workforce,
nor their cries for help issued to the state power. The strike was
for them more than a portent of what Cooke Taylor had called a
'NEW population' which 'must at some future and no distant
time, bear all the elements of society aloft upon its bosom'. The
determination and preparation of the government in 1848 when
the next upsurge of mass activity took place probably owed a great
deal to lessons learnt by the authorities in 1842.

From the workers' point of view a sense of alienation engendered
by employers and state may have found expression in the perhaps
surprising growth of trade unionism in the strike's aftermath.

Within two years of its end the colliers had established the first national mineworkers' association with the Staffordshire strikers of 1842 prominent. The collaboration of the Manchester metalworkers' societies in the strike led directly to the establishment of the forerunner of the Amalgamated Society of Engineers. The Potters' Union and the Cotton Spinners' Association were born in 1843 and the National Typographical Association in 1845. The tailors and shoemakers created new societies and likewise the United Flint Glassmakers' Society was established. None of this suggests that deep demoralisation flowed from defeat. On returning to the area in September 1842, Cooke Taylor said: 'The operatives are disappointed at the result of their late proceedings, but they are certainly not daunted; on the contrary, they boast of the great strength they displayed and the sympathy they met in almost every direction.'[41]

Though it may be fair to argue that the workers came out of the strike with a knowledge that they had only themselves to rely upon, they could not be said to have developed any clear philosophy around which to organise. There was a growing critique of life in an industrial capitalist society. At his trial at Lancaster Richard Pilling demonstrated this in his long defence. He detailed the evils of the system based on his own experience:

> over production; intolerably long hours of labour; competition and the beating down of wages; unemployment and poverty in the midst of plenty; the employment of child and juvenile labour and the break up of the family; lack of independence and control; the reification of human beings under commodity production; the many tyrannical and hypocritical actions of the cotton manufacturers – their insensitivity to the sufferings of operatives, blind adherence to the tenets of orthodox political economy, opposition to combination among workers and their frequent victimisation of labour activists ... and their abhorrence of Chartism.[42]

Arguments based on these concepts could not have been pursued 50 years earlier. Only the experience of a fully fledged capitalist industrial system could have taught them. So we have a comprehensive critique of the existing economic order and there is evidence that Pilling's was not a lone voice. However, the movement had not yet produced a 'working' alternative system of ideas beyond active trade unionism.

Though 1842 was a defeat, with terrible recriminations for masses of workers and their families, it had demonstrated the enormous potential power of the working class. It had released tremendous vigour, worker leadership and organisational versatility.

CHAPTER 4

Downturn 1842–47

In terms of militant activity of any kind the years between 1842 and 1848 were pretty dismal. The flat rejection, by the House of Commons, of the second mass petition, the defeat of the strike and the pursuit of activists by the authorities unquestionably created some fear and demoralisation among the rank and file, notwithstanding some impressive trade union growth. But furthermore, the grim starkness of life in the deep recession of 1841–42 gradually eased. Although its effects can easily be overestimated, the massive investment in railway-building characteristic of the mid-1840s did create a pick-up in economic activity and hence in employment. Railways were on the way to occupying their central role in the mid-Victorian economy stimulating growth in a wide range of industries including metal-working, coal-mining, civil engineering and building.

It would be crude and unsustainable to argue a straightforward match between rising living standards and declining political militancy from exploited groups. Indeed historically, rising living standards and a demand for labour have often had the opposite effect, whilst economic decline and unemployment have often led to workers' demoralisation. In this particular case what confidence might have risen from improved employment prospects was probably checked by the results of the defeat of 1842 and the consequent trials and sentences of the participants.

Nevertheless, the Chartists did not disappear in this period. If they had it is likely that the re-emergence of the mass movement in 1848 would not have taken place, for what is implicit in 1848 was the presence of a network of organisation and contacts which could be brought together rapidly. Of course tens of thousands must have gone to ground, beaten or waiting. Yet, although the circulation of the *Northern Star* tumbled from its heady heights of the summer of 1839, it had become firmly established in working-class communities and was to remain so throughout the 1840s, never falling below a weekly average of 6000 copies (based on stamp duty returns).[1]

Thousands became involved in other adjacent activities. Among the leaders to date, William Lovett and John Collins, released from gaol in July 1840, turned to a workers' educational project, ultimately called the National Association of the United Kingdom for Promoting the Social and Political Improvement of the People. It was seen by Lovett and his associates as an alternative to the O'Connor-led National Charter Association. Several leading London Chartists were drawn into this body which stressed progress for working men through self-improvement. It aimed to win the support of the middle classes by its insistence upon 'moral force'. The objects of this body were very fine. They included the establishment of circulating libraries,

> from a hundred to two hundred volumes each, containing the most useful works on politics, morals, the sciences, history ... [to] be sent in rotation from one town or village ... to erect public halls or schools for the people ... to be used during the day as infant, preparatory and high schools ... [where] the children shall be educated ... embracing physical, mental, moral and political instruction ... [in the evening] by adults for readings, discussions, musical entertainments, dancing ... such halls to have two commodious playgrounds ... a pleasure garden attached to each ... apartments for the teachers, rooms for hot and cold baths, for a small museum, a laboratory and general workshops where the members and their children may be taught experiments in science, as well as the first principles of the most useful trades ...[2]

Such schemes were much in advance of those devised after the coming of state education in the 1870s and in some respects would stand as a model for education even today. The main problem was that in a society so savagely marked along class lines they were frankly utopian. Their implementation would have required the sort of shake up of society that no one was yet contemplating. The mainstream activists were surely correct to see Lovett's initiative as a serious diversion from the Charter's main objectives.

Also released from gaol was Henry Vincent in January 1841. The 'tribune of the west' espoused the moral force position, aligned himself with Lovett and gradually turned his principal activity to the teetotal cause. Temperance was not without its attractions in a world where the appalling nature of life and work made alcohol a potent source of temporary release. Many political activists rightly saw booze as eroding the effectiveness of their activity.[3] However, as an alternative to the central struggle for universal suffrage, it too, was diversionary. Perhaps unsurprisingly, such Chartists, forswearing mass activity, were very welcome among liberal middle classes.

The liberal middle-class end of the movement, already shaken by the insurrectionary rhetoric and actions of the movement's mainstream, was increasingly drawn towards a moderation in agitational practice which would invite compromise on the Charter's six points. Such a body was the Complete Suffrage Union launched by the Quaker banker, Joseph Sturge, in Birmingham in 1841. Sturge and his associates, anxious to allay the fears of the middle classes, tried to concoct a programme which would divest the suffrage struggle of its associations with mass activity and violence. The conferences which were called, however, remained stubbornly attached to the concept of the Charter. The Complete Suffrage Union failed and its leaders failed in trying to build a bridge across the class divide. Nonetheless, this objective became an aim of almost all the national leaders of the movement in the 1840s.

One persistent difficulty with such cross-class alliances was the degree to which the Charter's objectives became vulnerable to pressure from other central preoccupations of the middle class in this period. This applied especially to the question of repeal of the Corn Laws. The issue had special resonance in south-east Lancashire where a confident factory and commercial bourgeoisie stood uncompromisingly for repeal as the cornerstone of their free trade philosophy but also as a potential panacea for their workforces demanding wage increases to meet the price of bread. Working-class Chartists were deeply suspicious of such motivations seeing, not middle-class friends of the people, but antagonistic employers. The *Manchester Guardian,* the mouthpiece of the free trade interest, was scathingly antagonistic to the Chartists. Accordingly Anti-Corn Law League meetings were constantly disrupted by Chartist hecklers. The possibility of useful collaboration was remote, yet a more sympathetic understanding did develop and Peel's Corn Law Repeal in 1846 was greeted with approval by most Chartist spokesmen.

The movement did fragment in this period as the petition campaigning foundered. Other Chartists moved into co-operation and trade unionism. In 1844 the Rochdale Co-operative initiative was launched by Chartist flannel weavers, and over the decade which followed the Rochdale practice was followed in many northern industrial communities. Former political activists were likely to play a leading role in such initiatives since they were often literate men with organising skills at something of a loose end as their political movement went into decline. There is a need to query, however, just how many of Chartism's working-class militants adopted this activity as a permanent diversion. Neville Kirk's recent study of post-Charter south-east Lancashire politics shows that whilst skilled workers, or former skilled workers, played an important role in the development of co-operation, there was a substantial influx of lower-middle-class elements, many of whom came to dominate the movement inculcating it with a middle-class value system.[4]

As we have seen above, trade unionism grew considerably after the mass strike and during the revival of trade. Chartists played an important role in this activity, including Martin Jude, the leader of the miners in the North-East. Whilst trade union organisation might have become a diversionary activity for some Chartist activists, it should be seen as a pursuit likely to assist keeping the ideas alive among workers. It could complement political activity. The Chartist trade unionist could earn the respect of his working colleagues by his dedication to trade union activity in an inclement climate. He might also be the seller of the *Northern Star,* thus helping to maintain a web of contacts for better days. O'Connor was certainly alive to the importance of the trade union link. It was always encouraged in the *Northern Star* and in 1844 the phrase *and National Trades Journal* was added to the title.

In the wake of the setbacks of 1839–40 and 1842 thousands of workers joined in a revived agitation for a reduction in working hours. Shorter working hours with the possibility of spreading work was an attractive proposition for a class dogged by mass unemployment in the early 1840s. Short Time Committees, dormant since the mid-1830s, sprang into life. Agitation was strongest in West Yorkshire among woollen workers led by the old Tory champion of factory reform, Richard Oastler. They held enormous meetings and petitioned Parliament, placing pressure upon the new Tory administration of Robert Peel. The status quo was defended fiercely by the factory owners and their greater pressure produced only a modest reform in the Ten Hours Act of 1847.[5]

So Chartists engaged in a wide variety of activities during the mid-1840s. Some more than others would lend the movement a continuity that was to be important when revival came about. Of all the activities, however, the most important was the Land Plan. It was the brainchild of Feargus O'Connor. He has been abused for his initiative by contemporaries and generations of historians. According to his critics the Land Plan was a utopian fantasy corrupted by poor organisation and financial incompetence, a diversion from the aims of the Charter.

Only recently have O'Connor's efforts been placed in a more objective perspective. The plan needs to be seen in its contemporary context. Land 'reform' had a long history in British radicalism.[6] In the 1840s there were thousands of workers who had arrived in their industrial settings as refugees from the brutal effects of enclosure or from the even more savage process of eviction in Ireland. The domination of land ownership by a tiny caste of hereditary aristocrats and gentry was a persistent theme in radical demonology. Life in the new industrial centres, whether town or village, was generally grim, intensified by the depredations of cyclical unemployment. The political fight for the Charter had provided a powerful focus between 1838 and 1842. Just how powerful is underlined by the thousands willing to risk life and limb in the face of rampant coercive state power. Parliament's arrogant rejection of petitioning and the failure of the Chartists' violent assaults against the authorities had brought the mass movement up against the limitations of its strategies. A breathing space would be required for recovery and possibly for a revaluation of those strategies.

It should not be surprising that a new direction, with great authority in radical tradition, should generate such enthusiasm. When it was presented by the figure of Feargus O'Connor, a figure almost deified amongst the workers, a man recently released from imprisonment for his convictions, it was irresistible. His leadership was reinforced because he was patently a man without cynicism. He believed in the project and unstintingly used his physical and financial resources to promote it. Some 70,000 men and women committed their meagre resources to a share in the plan, although only about 250 actually settled on the land. Half a dozen large estates were purchased and the smallholding enterprise was launched in 1845. Some of the cottages built on O'Connor's orders still stand in Hertfordshire and Worcestershire and have a quality unusual in early nineteenth-century workmen's dwellings.

It was not, however, a successful venture and had collapsed by 1851. It never had an administrative centre or accountancy procedures indispensable to efficient working. It was a financial disaster with most of the participants left penniless and destitute. The scheme was subject to a parliamentary enquiry which cleared Feargus O'Connor of corruption. What neither most contemporary critics nor subsequent historians were aware of was that the government had attempted to sabotage the scheme from the start. O'Connor was an ongoing target of ministers infuriated by his agitational activities throughout the period and particularly by his escape from severe penalties at his trial in 1843. During the period he campaigned vigorously and effectively for factory reform, against the workings of the New Poor Law, for trade union rights and against the Militia Bill of 1846, participating fully in the founding of a National Anti-Militia Association. He was a thorn in Whig flesh. His popular agitation eventually took him into Parliament for Nottingham in 1847 where he carried out a courageous one-man-band of opposition.

However, the Land Plan would have been likely to fail without government hostility or the organisational incompetence of its leaders. As a multitude of 'co-operative' enterprises have shown over the past 150 years, it is virtually impossible to build islands of non-capitalism (or even petty capitalism) in a capitalist society. Self-sufficiency can only go so far. Surplus produce needs to be produced to raise the money for tools, clothing and housing. It can only be sold at the prevailing market price which imposes certain conditions of labour upon the labourers. It usually demands an ongoing sacrifice for which the increased degree of autonomy can only sustain the morale for so long.

That it ended in catastrophe is undeniable but does not detract from the impact it made upon poor working people nor from the honourable intentions of its architect. It seems likely that engagement with the experiment held together a substantial part of the movement in the very difficult situation it faced after the defeats of 1842. We know from the extant records that the areas where the Land Plan won most adherents were the areas where Chartist organisation reacted most swiftly and effectively in the revival of 1848.

CHAPTER 5

1848

The British economy stumbled into a major commercial and financial crisis in the autumn of 1847 after three years of relative optimism during which investment in railways and railway-related activities had been colossal. Unemployment and starvation were again rampant, though not on the scale of the winter of 1841–42, except in Ireland which was experiencing its worst famine of the century after three consecutive failures of the potato crop. There was a stirring among Chartists and Irish nationalists. The death of Daniel O'Connell, an enemy of the Chartists since his refusal to defend trade union victims of the Whig reaction in the previous decade, opened up the possibility of a developing liaison. Despite O'Connell's position, there had been continuous Irish involvement in the Chartist movement, but his death, the intensification of Irish anger at British callousness to the effects of the famine and Feargus O'Connor's vituperative attacks on the government, inside and outside the House of Commons, gave the relationship a fresh impetus. Many Chartist associations were actually founded in Ireland. Then, in February 1848, the banner of revolution was raised in Paris. Soon a wave of rebellion swept across Europe.

Of English Chartist leaders, Julian Harney was the one with the most internationalist of outlooks. Close to Bronterre O'Brien, he had been attracted by his translation of Buonarotti's work published in 1837. He was the most influenced by Jacobinism, identifying himself with Marat, 'Thou whose imperishable title I have assumed'.[1] Imprisonment had taken many leading figures out of circulation in the early 1840s. Harney, who had escaped prison, had become sub-editor of the *Northern Star* and in 1844, with the movement already in decline, O'Connor had taken the paper from Leeds to London. Here Harney, appointed editor in 1845, worked closely with European émigrés, opening his columns to European issues. He wrote later, 'pains [were] taken to make the English democrat aware of the part that was being played by his brethren on the different stages of the political world'.[2] In September 1845 Harney and Ernest Jones, a new recruit to radical politics, co-operated with a group of European activists, including Frederick Engels and Karl Marx, to form the Fraternal Democrats. The close integration of leading Chartists into revolutionary European culture was of great significance. In 1848, excited by the news of February, the NCA sent a fraternal delegation (Harney, Jones and McGrath) to Paris and pledged to take the British popular movement down the same revolutionary road.

During the early spring meetings grew in size. Clearly the Chartist mass movement was on the way back. Large meetings were reported in the North and Scotland. In London a meeting of protest against taxation increases in Trafalgar Square was taken over by Chartists and a rash of window-breaking took place across central London. Serious riots also took place in Glasgow and in March some 20,000 people gathered on Kennington Common. The reconstituted Convention took the decision to launch a further petition and to call a mass meeting at Kennington for 10 April from which the demonstrators would march with the petition on Parliament.

The circulation of the *Northern Star* quickly climbed to double its average figure for the period 1843–47, but sales alone give no impression of its circulation. O'Connor, only slightly diverted from his new preoccupation, the Land Plan, was again on the stump speaking at mass meetings across the country. If O'Connor was still the charismatic figurehead of the movement, the new leader, intellectually and organisationally, was Ernest Jones. The son of an aristocratic family with royal connections, he was 29 in 1848 and was building an impressive reputation as a speaker and writer. He immediately identified with the militant physical force wing, which by 1848 was in the ascendant, the group round Lovett having drifted off into self-help activity. Emulation of the events in France was the initial stated objective of this new upsurge of activity. However, it was the old tactic of petitioning which was to form the centrepiece of early activity in the spring of 1848. The aim was to create a giant petition greater than those of the earlier stage of the movement, to assemble a massive force of people in London and to march with the petition on a Parliament which, it was hoped, would be cowed into acceptance.

Jones recommended an organisational refit of the movement into small activist sections. It certainly needed organisational revision since much of it had lain in tatters since 1842. The small section, or class, had an ambiguous genealogy. It could be seen to derive from the Jacobin clubs of revolutionary Paris in Year II of the great revolution, or from the highly successful Methodist classes organised in the industrial areas to efficiently implant the faith among the workers. Perhaps most Chartists in 1848 saw it in the former light, for primarily they appear to have seen a real need to build a defensive curtain against an anticipated bloody reaction from the state. It is not entirely clear what Ernest Jones thought on this matter for his speeches were loaded with ambiguity. On the one hand he proclaimed the need for preparations, whilst on the other forswore the use of violence.[3]

A similar conflict can be read in the words of O'Connor, too, in 1848. Active since the early 1830s, the experience of earlier struggles may have introduced considerable doubt in his mind as to the probable consequence of actions smacking of insurrection. He had already personally sampled the overweening power of the ruling class and was aware of the Russell government's ongoing preparations to deal with civil conflict. There was no sign whatever of a serious schism in that class, a split which might tear apart police and military. The opposite was the case. In fact Russell's government had given long and serious consideration to the issue. They were in a position to cash the credit built up with broad layers of the middle class after the concessions made to them in 1832 and subsequently through other important legislation. To a massive military force, thousands of pensioners and an adequately efficient police force, they were able to call upon tens of thousands of special constables who could be recruited, drilled and armed for potential conflict. The potential 'specials', recruited in droves in London, did not live or work face to face with proletarians as had been the case in the industrial areas in 1842. Accordingly there was no reluctance in their attitude. In fact the ability to rely upon this massive amateur force was especially important in 1848 given that Parliament also had to take into account the potential need for troops in Ireland, where smouldering Irish resentment might break out into violence. In the quieter climate of Ireland in 1842, the Peel government had been able to switch troops safely to the mainland.

Russell had also built up a most efficient spying system. Professional spies were important to penetrate the Chartist organisation but perhaps more important were the thousands of middle- and lower-middle-class informants in every region. By the time the sides were ranged against each other, the government's intelligence was very comprehensive. The government had a pretty good sense of the Chartist leadership's thinking and indeed at least in April did not really fear insurrection. What is more, by 1848 the government had at its disposal a growing railway system and the new electric telegraph.

Against this the Chartist opposition was inadequate. It did have its major asset: numbers. No one was quite clear how many, but probably the overwhelming majority of the industrial working class was Chartist, at least in inclination. There was also a rare daring and courage, as demonstrated in 1839 and 1842. The *Northern Star*, primarily, and other newspapers and journals were organisers in their own right, collecting and recording news of the struggle on a weekly basis and building a vast network of sellers and weekly discussion groups. This was less effective than in the early period, no doubt, but still a significant factor in the building of Chartist confidence. The national leaders were effective orators capable of rousing passions in masses of workers and no one doubted their sincerity and willingness to sacrifice themselves. There was also a range of local leaders, most having served prison sentences between 1839 and 1844. This was a smaller group than it might have been, since imprisonment and transportation had taken a considerable toll. It is also apparent that many had emigrated to seek a better life elsewhere.

Perhaps the biggest problem for the Chartists, though, was not the power of the state, formidable though that certainly was, but the strategic uncertainties of the leadership. In the ascendant throughout the period was a strategy based on a mixture of English radicalism and French Jacobinism: crudely, the mass platform, petition and armed insurrection. As means of breaching state power all were useless. They belonged fundamentally to a different kind of society. They had been deployed with some success in the previous decade for parliamentary reform and Catholic emancipation but in both cases there was strong support within Parliament and in the middle class outside. In the Chartist period only a handful of MPs supported the six points and the middle class was solidly behind the government.

Platform and the petition could have had the purpose simply of providing an agitational and organisational focus for Chartist activists, but to sow illusions that large meetings and enough signatures could force a government, indeed an entrenched ruling class, to change its attitude on what it saw as a fundamental principle affecting its survival, was really naive.

Of course many Chartists saw this perfectly clearly. This perception was probably what drew them to the physical force solution of either massive street demonstrations or the arming of a proto-National Guard (the nomenclature of 1848) for an assault on real or symbolic targets associated with state or municipal power. It is likely that so long as the ruling class remained united, the mass demonstration could never be 'mass' enough to shake the government. Perhaps some Chartists hoped for an assault by the military or police which would stir the masses into a violent rage. However this did not happen, at least partly because a confident ruling class was enough in command of intelligence to know that a firm demonstration of overwhelming force was less risky than bodies in the street. Crucially the major military commanders, Sir Charles Napier and Sir Thomas Arbuthnot, clearly understood this and it was never lost sight of by men like Russell and Grey. Even the belligerent Duke of Wellington demonstrated such understanding in 1848.[4] The rulers had also learnt earlier the efficacy of drawing back from the brink of ultimate punishment, presented of course as clemency, not weakness. The treatment of Frost, Williams and Jones in 1840 and O'Connor and associates in 1843 has this flavour about it.

Neither was the armed band solution likely to be effective. Firstly it would require arming on a scale probably well beyond the movement in the 1840s. We know that some arming took place. Pikes were made in backyard furnaces in the Midlands, South Wales and the North. In this period it was a primitive weapon and effective in hand-to-hand combat, but not able to stand up to strafing by modern guns including small field pieces. Guns were in circulation but had to be purchased from gunsmiths, most of whom were unsympathetic to Chartists or under the surveillance of the government. Relatively few appear to have fallen into Chartist hands. To be effective would have meant seizing armouries and winning over sections of the troops. There is no evidence of the Chartists getting anywhere near these two objectives.

Then there was the problem that for such assaults to be effective would mean simultaneous attacks in different parts of the country and crucially in the capital. Although there is a little evidence that some were aware of this requirement and perhaps had some rudimentary plans laid, the scale appears to have been incommensurate with the enormity of the task. Government communications on the other hand were already pretty sophisticated. The Chartists would have required the organisation and centralised leadership of a revolutionary party to have made such a tactic viable and understood throughout the movement.

The national leaders of the movement always appear to have had a basic understanding that whilst, according to their viewpoint, physical force might have moral right on its side, it was not likely to be carried out on a scale great enough to win and impose a new order upon society. However, this needs to be seen in its context. There was a means for the Chartist movement to have carried out a much more effective campaign. This was glimpsed briefly in the mass strike of 1842. There does appear to have been a moment in that summer when workers' actions shook the government. The mass strike carried out by giant flying pickets was effective and difficult to deal with. It had the potential to operate on many fronts, more or less simultaneously, and for a limited time it did just that. It was very effective in the south-east Lancashire of factory operatives working in enterprises with substantial numbers of workers, but ultimately less so in the West Yorkshire territory of small workshops. And it was here that the spreading movement ground to a halt in set-piece confrontations with the military just outside Leeds. The older tactic came to the fore again and was once more proved ineffective.

It is of course spurious to criticise with hindsight. The activities of 1842 were a great potential learning experience. There is not much evidence from the Chartist press that much took place beyond the already canvassed notion that unarmed or poorly armed workers had little chance against trained soldiers, especially when those soldiers remained loyal to the state. This latter point was an important lesson too, for there had been an often made but unsubstantiated claim that the 'other ranks' were 'Chartists' waiting to rebel. Again, the evidence of this is very thin indeed.[5] It is clear that whilst all the national leaders of the movement in 1848 appear to have fully absorbed these points from previous encounters, there was little evidence of discussion of an alternative tactic, other than back to petitioning. Whilst there was creeping into the movement, by 1848, a sense of a need to attach social and economic objectives to the Charter, there seems little grasp of the working class as having a massive potential strength deriving from its role at the point of production.

The great set-piece confrontation took place on 10 April 1848. In a sense it was a set-piece because the government decided it should be so. In effect they engineered it by propaganda. The Chartist leadership organised for a peaceful and unarmed rally at Kennington which would then send a mass delegation bearing the petition to Parliament. It is true that many Chartists feared state butchery but to an extent this emanated from the massive and obvious preparations which the government was seen to be making for an event of quite a different character, egged on by a nearly hysterical press. We know what the Chartists could not know: that Russell and colleagues were well aware of the real relations of forces. On the day the Chartist leaders were completely boxed in and had to try to make the best of an awful situation. In the face of overwhelming force and the absolute arrogance of the state and its supporters, they actually behaved with considerable dignity. Feargus O'Connor was even able to claim a victory, though perhaps with no great conviction. That the picture of rout presented to posterity was not one immediately perceived by the movement is strongly suggested by the fact that in the months which followed that day, the provincial movement actually grew.

The government, in its private councils, was by no means convinced of its triumph. Throughout the spring and summer it was preoccupied by the fear of the Irish nationalist and mainland Chartist movements combining to threaten the stability of the state, perhaps stimulated by the frequent news of deep unrest in Europe. There was special concern for those areas of the mainland which contained the largest number of Irish immigrants. That south-east Lancashire was both the area with the greatest concentration of Irish workers and one where there was a distinct revival of Chartism weighed heavily on men who remembered 1842. The government decided on a pre-emptive strike upon the movement, detaining the national leaders and rooting out the most active of the rank and file. The crucial constitutional back-up was the 'Gagging Act' and the Aliens Act. The former introduced the offence of treason-felony which carried the punishment of seven years' prison to transportation for life. The latter gave the Home Secretary the right to deport any foreigner whose presence was deemed likely to disturb the peace of the realm. The Fraternal Democrats felt the threat so keenly that they actually dissolved themselves in May.

The defeat of the petitioning tactic had left the national leadership marooned without an effective policy beyond the attempt to constitute a National Assembly in place of the Convention. In the face of the government clampdown such a public demonstration of potential subversion of the constitution was certain to be ineffective. The only direction left for the most determined provincial Chartists was to prepare for armed insurrection.

The summer was marked by reports of arming and drilling, by mass meetings and violent clashes with the authorities in Glasgow, Aberdeen, Bradford, Leicester, Manchester, Ashton-under-Lyne, and London where the movement recovered from 10 April to the extent of managing to mount a march of some 80,000 workers in May, only two days after 2000 Bradford Chartists had fought successfully with police and special constables. At least part of the context for this upsurge in activity was a reaction to the harsh sentence of 14 years' transportation upon John Mitchell who was accused of fomenting rebellion in Ireland.

Part of the London movement turned to clandestine plans for insurrection in August, an adventure which seems to have had some support in Lancashire and the West Riding. Penetrated by spies, the movement was hopelessly vulnerable to the massive government assault which was stepped up from June to August. Some 266 persons were committed for seditious offences largely on the evidence of spies and informers. Many were transported, most were imprisoned. The movement's left wing was rendered virtually leaderless nationally and locally. Ernest Jones, the most prominent leader indicted, received a two-year sentence for using seditious language. Deprived of reading and writing materials, he was vindictively treated, emerging physically weak but ready to carry on the struggle having moved intellectually from republicanism to socialism.

By the autumn the mass movement was dead. Uncertain tactics, divided leadership, and a wily and united government demonstrating huge force backed by a confident middle class, undermined the movement's brief upsurge. Chartism survived for a further decade.

It was a smaller movement meeting largely indoors rather than the moors and streets, with the notable, if localised, exception of the great Preston textile strike in 1853–54. The insurrectionary wing was almost dead. Feargus O'Connor's great land experiment crashed in 1851, ultimately halted by a hostile Parliament and courts. Campaigns for Parliament and local councils became the main order of the day. Some survivors slipped into middle-class non-universalist suffrage campaigns like the Little Charter and the National Parliamentary and Financial Reform Association.

Despite violent disagreements between mainstream leaders, both personal and political, greater theoretical clarity was introduced by figures like Ernest Jones in association with Marx, Engels and other European émigrés. A socialist programme was adopted at the National Charter Association's Manchester Conference in 1851. It was formally carried forward by its offspring, the Labour Parliament founded in 1854. It was to little effect. Working-class Chartism, the vital ingredient in any revival, was shell-shocked by the slicing off of its local leadership and intimidated into passivity. By the time psychological recovery could take place, economic life was on an upswing. The desperate constituency of outworkers had dwindled, its survivors either totally marginalised or integrated into the factory and workshop. A small, though vulnerable space was available for the development of craft trade unionism, a slightly less threatened one for active co-operation. Then there was the slow emergence of a liberalism open to the careerist impulses of some working-class politicos. Even a figure as principled as Jones was ultimately drawn in that direction.

CHAPTER 6

Anatomy of the Movement

Members

Quantification of the movement has always been very difficult. From estimates of attendance at the great mass meetings in 1839 and 1848, we can safely assume hundreds of thousands of supporters. The peak sale of the *Northern Star* was registered at 50,000. Since many were sold on the streets and in the pubs many readers were probably buying casually and not every time. Since we also know that copies were passed around many hands the readership may well have exceeded 200,000. For membership, since there are very few extant lists, we are reduced to intelligent guesswork. Dorothy Thompson's excellent table of locations and activities indicates that there were approaching 1000 places in which some kind of activity took place.[1] They cover virtually every region of Britain. We also have lists of those buying into the Land Company amounting to some 70,000. It is hard to imagine any but the most geographically isolated working-class community being completely untouched by Chartism, illustrating the centrality of this movement in the development of class consciousness across the whole working class.

It was a working-class movement with middle-class adherents. It is true that a chunk of the Birmingham middle class was instrumental in providing a focus for the formulation of the People's Charter. The majority of the delegates to the National Convention were from lower-middle-class occupations. Most of the best known national leaders also came from this social stratum. A substantial number of such people pulled away from the movement after the first signs of militancy, and after Newport the survivors of this group were largely full-time adherents of militant radicalism and Jacobinism. Of course the term working class as applied to those who laboured for wages in the period covered an immense variety of experience, from those still struggling in forms of outwork to those employed in sizeable factories. The Charter's objectives were what united such disparate elements. But even so, such unity was only evident for brief moments like the run up to the first Convention, the period round the presentation of the second petition and mass strike in 1842, and perhaps in the spring and summer of 1848.

Unity and coherence have often been questioned. It has been suggested that the bulk of participants were displaced outworkers and that factory and other larger workshop employees did not become involved. The number of outworkers identified in written records may suggest a disproportionate involvement but might also reflect individual histories of past radical activity, religious non-conforming organisational experience and higher than average levels of literacy. There isn't much dispute that the pool of London activists contained many lower-middle-class radicals and skilled tradesmen: the men who attended meetings, wrote articles and sold newspapers. However, when the movement took to the streets in the spring and summer of 1842 and in 1848 it is reasonable to presume that the constituency was very much wider, taking in riverside workers, general labourers and the unemployed.

It is evident from the mass signings up in South Wales in the summer of 1839 that Chartism cut with the grain among the 'new' proletarians of coal and iron and that in the Midlands and North in 1842 it was factory and large workshop operatives who formed the mass meetings and flying pickets which linked the Charter's objectives to the struggle to resist wage cutting. Indeed, whenever there is evidence of mass attendance at meetings it would be inconceivable to imagine the bulk of those present being anything else but proletarians. Colliers, ironworkers and riverworkers, for example, must have formed the largest contingents of the 40,000 on Newcastle Town Moor to hear Harney on New Year's Day 1839. That was what the greatest number of Tyneside workers did at that time. The same must have been true at Peep Green, Kersal Moor, Glasgow Green, Mottram Moor and Woodhouse Moor.

It was the mass involvement of industrial workers which made the movement threatening to the ruling class except in London where it was the casual poor. The dissident middle-class elements and the skilled craftsmen were more familiar to the ruling circles. They could be engaged in serious discussion, or patronised, but not so the massed ranks of workers. They made local magistrates, army commanders and politicians anxious as private and public comments make clear, and within the working-class ranks the Irish were a particular worry. In 1836 an employer giving evidence to a parliamentary commission said: 'where there is discontent, or a disposition to combine, or turn outs among the work people, the Irish are the leaders; they are the most difficult to reason with and convince on the subject of wages and regulations in factories'.[2]

There has, however been confusion amongst historians about the Irish influence on Chartism. After he was denounced by O'Connor and O'Brien, Daniel O'Connell tried to prevent Irishmen participating in the movement. Irish organisations and the Catholic hierarchy diligently backed him. That this pressure had considerable

effect is indisputed. On the other hand it is significant that below
the national leadership, which included the Irishmen O'Connor and
O'Brien, local leaderships in the regions contained many Irishmen
who seemingly ignored the instruction to stay away from the
Chartists. Many had long radical credentials which may have
placed them beyond the influence of middle-class leaders and
church. The issues which caused the split were the anti-Poor Law
movement and the campaign to free the Glasgow Cotton Spinners,
some of whom were Irish anyway. The hatred of the British state
was likely to carry at least as much weight as Whiggish political
economy and anti-trade unionism. The likely veracity of this
argument is at least suggested by the lists of prisoners committed
by the state, in each of the purges. They contain Irishmen in
numbers far greater than their proportion in the population. There
is also the strong circumstantial evidence of areas with large
immigrant Irish populations being the ones where Chartism made
the greatest impact. One of the most vigorous and effective organisers
in Leeds, Birmingham, Manchester and Bradford was George
White, a former woolcomber who served three prison sentences in
the 1840s. William Ashton of Barnsley, the weaver son of Irish
parents, was a delegate to the Convention and apparently one of
the organisers of the proposed rising which was to have been
triggered by the events in South Wales. Ashton had just returned
from Tasmania where he had been transported in 1830 for
involvement in both a weavers' strike and a riot at Dodworth. His
co-defendant Frank Mirfield was also Irish. A leading figure in
Stockport in the preparations for the mass strike of 1842 was
another Irishman, Thomas Clark. In a speech in July of that year
he argued,

> if they had repeal of the union tomorrow, with the present
> franchise, they would be little or no better off ... How many times
> have we been made to throw up our cawbeens and shillelahs
> and give three cheers for the Queen and the best ministry
> Ireland ever saw ... I ask you my fellow countrymen, what have
> Irish Catholic members done for us?[3]

All four appear to be exactly the kind of men unlikely to listen to
a cardinal or an O'Connell.

O'Connell's death in 1847 coincided with one of the bleakest
moment in Irish history. Potato famine, accelerating evictions from
the land and a step up in violence from the state produced a
growing stream of migrants from Ireland to the industrial areas of
Britain. Such migrants brought with them first-hand experience of
the sheer cruelty of the colonial relationship. There is plenty of
evidence of Irish involvement in the rebellious sentiment of such
areas in the spring and summer of 1848.

Two of the three men tried, convicted and transported to Tasmania for life for their leading role in the abortive London rising of August were Irish. They were Thomas Fay and William Lacey. The third was the remarkable figure of William Cuffey, a 61-year-old black tailor, elected President of the Metropolitan District Council of Chartists.

The Irishmen and the black man can stand as an interesting symbol of the force of mass movements of rebellion to overcome violent prejudice. Real or alleged ethnic differences were a persistent source of division in the working-class movement. Anti-Irish sentiment ran back at least into the eighteenth century. Although antagonism was much intensified after the famine and mass migration of the 1840s, the Irish with their extraordinary capacity to fight against their awful oppression were long hated with special intensity by their oppressors. Among workers, fear was fanned that migration would 'reduce the labouring classes to a uniform state of degradation and misery'.[4] And employers regularly used migrants as strike-breakers to weaken workers' resistance. However, it was probably that fighting spirit, allied to great courage and daring, that earned Irishmen respect in a movement struggling to bring citizenship to working people.

There had been a long association of anti-slavery sentiment and radical politics in Britain. In the 1830s, however, just at the point where the abolitionists were to achieve their goal of outlawing slavery in the British empire, an uneasy relationship developed between that movement and working-class radicals. Some of the most determined abolitionists were also advocates of the New Poor Law, hostile to factory reform and trade unionism. Some radicals who were to become Chartists were quick to make the point that it was hypocritical to advocate the end of black slavery whilst resisting reforms which could relieve the plight of 'wage slaves'. When the abolitionists turned their campaigning to the situation in the United States this ambivalence was to remain. Uneasy about trade unionism and supportive of the New Poor Law, many middle-class abolitionists associated with the middle-class suffrage campaigns which emerged in competition with the National Charter Association in the 1840s. Nevertheless, figures like O'Brien, Harney and Jones associated with visiting American abolitionists like Frederick Douglass. Jones maintained his interest in the issue right up to the period of the American Civil War.

Women played an important part in the Chartist movement. Though we know of none who attained leadership roles nationally or locally, they were reported to be in the front line, against the soldiers' bayonets in the demonstration at Halifax in August 1842. There are also fleeting glimpses of women activists at Barnsley, Bradford, Sheffield, Ashton, the Potteries and east London. There

are records of nearly 100 associations of female radicals during the
Chartist period and women participated as ordinary members in
many branches and thousands of women signed the petitions. At
its peak moments Chartism was a family and community
organisation in which 'everybody' participated. Where action
directly flowed from mass meetings it is likely that women
participated fully. This would be true of big turn-outs like 1842
where young women formed a substantial part of the factory labour
force in Lancashire and the Potteries and probably also of mass
petitioning where all hands could be put to use. On the other
hand, smaller indoor gatherings where resolutions were prepared
and delegates frequently elected proceedings were likely to be
dominated by experienced and usually older males. (*Young* men
may have 'suffered' the same inclusion and exclusion.) The *Northern
Star* reported from Bradford in 1839:

> The female radicals of the Bradford district, amounting to
> upward of 600, walked in procession through the principal
> streets headed by a band of music and banners ... at the head
> of the procession there was carried by a woman a large printed
> board with the words 'exclusive dealing'...[5]

Monitoring the shops under the Convention's 'exclusive dealing'
policy was likely to be an activity carried out by housewives,
reinforcing the impression of Chartism as a movement in which
everyone could find a useful place.

There is also plenty of evidence that male activists did believe
in women's suffrage. Some explicitly made their position clear and
campaigned for it, including R. J. Richardson who wrote a pamphlet
arguing for it:

> I shall now proceed to the main feature of the question ...
> 'Ought women to interfere in the political affairs of the country?'
> ... I do most distinctly and unequivocally say – YES! And for
> the following reasons:
> *First,* because she has a natural right.
> *Second,* because she has a civil right.
> *Third,* because she has a political right.
> *Fourth,* because it is a duty imperative upon her.
> *Fifthly,* because it is derogatory to the divine will to neglect so
> imperative a duty.[6]

Women's suffrage was also said to have been included in the early
drafts of the Charter but removed for fear of alienating potential
supporters. Whether or not this was an accurate assessment of its
fate, it is clear that even advocating women's rights was an advanced
position in a society where women had no formal rights of citizenship.
It also seems to be the case that women's involvement in Chartism

through mass activity was a high point of women's involvement in public affairs, for, from the late 1840s, the drive to assert the central role of women in nurturing a wholesome family life became ascendant. Only a militant mass movement was likely to mount a serious challenge to the ideological barrage issued by pulpit, press and politician. After 1848 such movements were gone for at least a generation.[7]

Ideas and strategies

The failure of the Chartists to win their demands, indeed to dent the confidence of the rulers, has always provoked a debate among historians. In recent times the failure has been attributed to the movement's failure to develop a coherent set of ideas appropriate to a workers' movement: that it could not escape the dominance of some of the main themes of eighteenth-century radicalism and its animus to Old Corruption.[8] A lack of coherence *is* evident, but, within limits, the struggle for the six points provided the focus. Nevertheless, as argued above, strategies for advance were found wanting at the high points of militant activity. Ideological diversity could have a schismatic effect, especially in the troughs of activity, but to attribute the movement's failures to programmatic or theoretical weakness is far too monocausal to maintain credibility.

Stedman Jones has counselled the down-playing of class position in understanding Chartism, in effectively trying to uncouple social position and the language employed by activists.[9] He is on very thin ice. Social class location was crucial in what people brought to Chartism,[10] just as it was in the powerful forces which opposed it. The first crop of radicals who broke with radical Whigs during and after the Reform Bill crisis were reacting strongly to members of the more prosperous middle class who wanted to halt the trajectory of reform because they felt that their property was threatened by both militant unconstitutional tactics and the entry to political discourse and activity of propertyless proletarian masses.

That the first crop of Chartists were often petite bourgeois journalists, attorneys, shopkeepers, booksellers and highly skilled artisans is very much to the point. Many were marginal members of middle-class society in terms of wealth and social standing. Even if some of them might have scraped onto the electoral register after 1832, they were still aware of a strong sense of powerlessness in relation to the big bourgeoisie and aristocracy. Also many small businessmen, and especially shopkeepers, were dependent on workers for their livelihood. Many were former workers sharing living space and cultural practices with workers. This was a stratum whose political credentials reached back into the eighteenth century and whose Paineite and Jacobin sensibilities were entirely understandable in class terms with their strong identification with the 'little man'.

Similarly the displaced handicraft workers, truly marginalised by the progress of capitalist technology and organisation, were often influenced by the communitarian vision of Thomas Spence and Robert Owen. In desperate straits, occasioned by the periodic crises, they could easily weld their utopianism onto Jacobinism, making them strong candidates for the insurrectionary road. Cotton operatives, colliers and metalworkers, many of whom by the late 1830s were working in workspaces of more than a hundred, were inevitably becoming at least dimly aware of their latent power at work as a contrast to its total absence in society at large. Some could have ideological standpoints like the petit bourgeois elements and the handicraft workers, but, accompanied by a basic trade union consciousness, there could develop the confidence to reach out for power, by striking or moving towards insurrection. Together, these elements could be a most potent cocktail in which class origins and class location were quite simply inseparable from the ideologies espoused. We don't only have isolated examples of these tendencies to draw upon either. As we have seen above, most of them were present in each region or area in which the Chartists operated.

The language spoken and written is of some use to us in understanding motivation and intention, providing we register both the origins and authority of the speaker and the context in which the words were spoken.[11] Furthermore, its usefulness is limited by such matters as the partiality of scribes, the presence of spies, and the weighting of what survives towards the literate and, usually, middle class. It has been suggested that as much might be learnt by the study of the use of symbols such as flags, banners and clothing.[12]

The moral force–physical force division has been considered decisive in understanding the social character of the movement. 'Moral force' indicated the strong influence of middle-class and artisan ideas and personnel, 'physical force' indicated the untutored rawness of the new proletariat. Since moral force arguments tended to dominate the movement, it might be concluded that this is evidence of the continued strength of middle-class and artisan ideas at the expense of the proletarian, an indication therefore of the underdeveloped character of this class. Such an argument has some force but also problems.

There were middle-class radicals and workers arguing both positions in the movement. Whilst the majority of those participating in physical force activities were certainly workers, middle-class radicals probably predominated among the *spokesmen* for these actions. Perhaps they represented the declining impact of Jacobinism as much as prefiguring proletarian insurrection. An argument for proletarian insurrection, as against people's insurrection, would have been oriented much more upon the workplace and a sense of workers' potential power. Most of the militant outbreaks, though usually strongly proletarian in composition, do not appear to have considered the importance of using workers' economic strength to bring the system to a halt. Rather, they were concerned to seize symbols of ruling-class power by armed force, such as at Newport, Llanidloes, Sheffield and Bradford. There were strikes of course, but they seem to have been largely perceived as a means to achieve the freedom to march, demonstrate and, perhaps, use arms. Though the proposed 'sacred month' was obviously a political strike, there was little evidence of even a rudimentary call for workers' control.

The strikes of 1842 may be considered as a special case as industrial power was central. They started as a resistance to savage wage cutting. Since many of the leading militants were Chartists it is not surprising that the call for implementation of the Chartist demands should have been made. The idea was certainly introduced that a mass strike could force the government to concede: the idea of 'sacred month'.[13] But again, there is no evidence of an explicit sense that workers could go farther than achieving the vote, though in some vague way perhaps the achievement of the suffrage could give workers access to the affairs of state. Of course the idea of workers' power was an argument as yet unknown to participants in the 1830s. Nevertheless, an insurrection based upon street conflict with police and soldiers, with scant attention to the immobilising of industry,[14] owes more to Jacobinism than a confidence in the industrial power of the working class.

Another problem is suggested. Did the advocacy of the use of industrial power in pursuit of the Charter make a man or woman a physical or moral force Chartist? It is clear from the evidence that advocates of the 'sacred month' or 'national holiday', whilst tending to the physical force position, could see themselves as belonging to either wing. Some saw it presaging a counterattack by the state which would lead to a general uprising, whilst others apparently imagined the government would just concede the suffrage.

Though the middle class, as a social force, might be more amenable to the moral force argument, it does not seem to be a specifically middle-class argument, as the subsequent history of working-class reformism seems to suggest. Even then, the argument falls into a rather static view of consciousness which is not warranted by the evidence. Class consciousness should not be seen as equating with revolutionary consciousness. Indeed revolutionary consciousness itself is problematic. The 'Jacobin' could demonstrate revolutionary consciousness in his desire for a vanguard to seize power through insurrection, regardless of the weight of the social

base on which the action was to be founded. But so could those
rooted in the organisations of the working class who argued, from
knowledge of the class, that such an action was an adventure
incapable of success *at that time*. This was the position taken up
by that most Jacobin of Chartists, Julian Harney, in August 1842.
Returning from the National Charter Association meeting in
Manchester, which had supported the mass strike then in progress,
he argued with the Sheffield workers against joining the strike. His
grounds were that in a confrontation with the military, at that
time, the workers' movement would be destroyed. A much greater
level of Chartist organisation was required. The situation was
complex.

These complexities are hinted at in a number of local studies where
local movements are seen to shift in their positions. At the
Convention of 1839 the old leadership of the Birmingham Political
Union took themselves out of the movement. Their secession has
been seen as a response to the moral force–physical force controversy.
Dorothy Thompson, however, shows that we need careful
assessment of its significance:

> The Birmingham delegates were by March something of an
> anachronism. They were not individual members of the middle
> class who happened to have radical views, but the representa-
> tives of a city and a class which was, for the moment in opposition
> to the Whigs, but which was in no way in sympathy with the
> radicalism of even its own city's artisan and working class.[15]

The movement in the Black Country, the Potteries, Sheffield and
South Yorkshire and Tyneside was also full of ambiguities. It
shifted from militancy to moderation in response to circumstances,
as much as social origins. The upturns in militancy in 1839 and
1842, for example, followed frustration at the outright rejection of
the petitions by Parliament. The downturns in the autumns of 1839
and 1842 and again in 1848, are surely not unconnected to the
government's successful beheading of the movement nationally and,
perhaps more crucially, locally, by mass arrests, to say nothing of
the gyrations in the economy.

Chartism can be seen as a transitional movement, a critical
meeting point of two political traditions. On the one hand there
was a people's politics of cross-class coalition where the interests
and outlooks of the middle classes usually dominated because
working-class organisation was weak and underdeveloped. Such
politics covered a wide spectrum from the radical end of
parliamentary politics to an underground of 'primitive communism',
romantic yearnings for an allegedly 'better' past, and satirical and
pornographic unstamped journalism. Tactics ranged from the
mass platform and petition to pike-making and drilling for proposed

insurrection. On the other hand there was a new tradition of workers' politics where, although middle-class people might participate and even lead, workers' participation and interests came to the fore. In terms of ideas it was characterised by various brands of utopianism, an internationalist perspective and eventually social democracy. Here stable organisation, with branches, subscriptions, delegation, open propaganda in mass meetings and the press, and the political strike became part of the political agenda. Chartism did not achieve clarity in either ideas or strategy until perhaps its declining years in the 1850s when the movement was won for social democracy. Nevertheless, to characterise the movement as hobbled by its adherence to eighteenth-century radicalism, as does Stedman Jones, is both wide of the mark in terms of its variety of ideas and attributes too much autonomy to ideas themselves.

The press and the leadership

The launching of the *Northern Star* by O'Connor's own efforts and finance, and putting it at the disposal of the movement, was an inspiration. It was not the first paper to report on the struggles of the working class but it was in many ways a pioneering enterprise. At its peak it enjoyed a sale of 50,000 copies but its message may have reached four or five times that number. The best radical journalists of the period wrote for the paper, including Bronterre O'Brien, a man of theoretical sophistication, who was regarded as the movement's finest communicator of ideas. The paper was accessible to all literate working men, but was written in a style which made it ideal for reading aloud to intent circles gathered for the purpose.[16] Consulting almost any issue of the paper shows that working men felt the confidence to write their own pieces to join in the day's controversies. But it was much more than a paper of controversy. It carried detailed and regular reports on local strikes and other working men's activities.

Historians have accused O'Connor of wantonly imposing his vision upon the movement. It is an accusation which does no justice to his contribution to the paper. As proprietor he could have imposed his will arbitrarily upon the *Northern Star*. Yet none of his editors remarked on his interference, even when they had left the paper and become hostile critics. Although he did spend periods in the office it was much more characteristic for him to be on the road speaking to working-class audiences. In fact it was probably his persistent contact with the readers which gave the paper its marvellous sensitivity to working-class moods and attitudes. Furthermore, all of the great controversies which were part of

Chartism's history were carried by the paper, usually giving fair coverage to all sides.

After the collapse of the strikes in the summer of 1842 and the trials which followed in the autumn and spring of 1843, the movement went into a decline. Opponents took the opportunity to revive interest in reform less than universal suffrage. Middle-class elements tried to forge a link with Anti-Corn Law politics and others with the growing temperance movement. It was O'Connor more than anyone who insisted upon maintaining Chartism's integrity as a workers' movement orienting attention firmly upon workers' issues, and in particular the struggles to develop trade unionism in a number of industries. With the NCA battered and demoralised by the attacks of the state, the *Northern Star* provided the movement's effective leadership. Still eagerly awaited weekly, in working-class communities the paper provide a national perspective, a focus of activity, news of successes in the localities, opinion on the great questions of the day and a political lead to the movement. And it was O'Connor's paper.

In the downturn following the defeats of 1842, O'Connor more than any other major leader saw that it was essential to maintain the movement's working-class orientation but his intense pursuit of this goal led the movement into a serious blind alley: the Land Plan. Building a 'new' society for workers on the basis of peasant proprietorship was something of a hobby horse of O'Connor, but it was also a virile strand in British radical politics, represented in different forms by Thomas Spence, William Cobbett and Robert Owen. The latter's ideas had received a favourable airing in the *Northern Star*. In the mid-1840s amidst mass unemployment, short time and restructuring of industry involving further disaster for handworkers, such ideas cut with the grain among the oppressed. The other unappealing alternatives on offer were Corn Law reform (seen as a bosses' project) and emigration. So, in the eyes of many workers, O'Connor's plan, backed with his own money, was not seen as a madcap scheme.

Despite his election to Parliament for Nottingham in 1847, a startling success in itself,[17] he was to play a declining part in the movement after 1848 when he presented the third petition to Parliament, proclaiming that 'our movement is a labour movement, originated in the first instance by fustian jackets, the blistered hands and the unshorn chins'.[18] He came out of the 10 April affair and the attack on the Land Plan disoriented and probably by that time in the early stages of mental illness. He did not participate in the movement's central council, deprecating its swing to explicit socialism. Relinquishing his ownership of the *Northern Star* in 1851, he died in 1855 after a period in an asylum.

O'Connor was certainly the movement's most outstanding leader and one who stayed the pace despite arrests, trials, prison and the regular hostility of the ruling class until illness took over. There were other talented figures, such as O'Brien,[19] a man of ideas; Harney, an intrepid organiser and talented journalist; Vincent, a brilliant orator; Cooper, indefatigable traveller and speaker; McDouall, almost pre-Bolshevik in his enthusiasm for creating a workers' vanguard; and Jones, who is most clearly identified with the socialist politics developed after 1848. O'Brien, Harney and Jones can be regarded as the leaders who took the movement towards socialism, though perhaps a majority of the first cohort of working-class Chartist activists would have thought of themselves as socialists. O'Brien, as early as 1834, argued that:

> universal suffrage can be of little use, if applied only to political purposes. In fact it is only as an auxiliary to social reform, or as a means of protecting the multitude in the establishment of new institutions for the production and distribution of wealth, that universal suffrage would develop its virtues.[20]

Attracted by the co-operative ideas of Robert Owen, O'Brien took the ideas onto a different plain by arguing, against Owen, that socialism required a political dimension. The 'utopia' could not be built without working people gaining command of the state. Since he also admired Robespierre, his politics were an amalgamation of Owenism and Jacobinism and initially took him onto the physical force wing of Chartism. Although his influence on the Chartist movement declined after his period of imprisonment which ended in 1841, he remained an active socialist, forming the National Reform League in 1849. It was from his circle in central London that the only real connection of Chartism with revived social democracy was made in the 1880s. The O'Brienites were generally well regarded by Marx who, although pouring scorn upon O'Brien's advocacy of currency reform, valued their participation in the General Council of the First International in the 1860s:

> These O'Brienites, in spite of their follies, constitute an often necessary counterweight to trade unionists in the Council. They are more revolutionary, firmer on the land question, less nationalistic, and not susceptible to bourgeois bribery in one form or another.[21]

Most of the London artisans hammering out the points in the People's Charter were also socialists, though those round Lovett were not drawn by Jacobin ideas, their Owenism leading much more towards the politics of steady persuasion. Many shrank from the notion of insurrection and several, including Lovett, withdrew from the mainstream of the movement after they were released from prison, turning their attention to workers' self-improvement through education.

For Harney, Jacobinism was rather stronger than socialism at the point where he helped found the East London Democratric Association. On his early tours the thrust of his speeches was an argument for action combined with radical rather than socialist politics. The experience of the abortive insurrectionary activity of 1839–40 seemed to lead him to a considerable revision of his position, but it is likely that he was also influenced by his period as an organiser among the workers of Sheffield. As we have seen, he certainly shrank from leading those workers against the bayonets of the military during the mass strike of 1842. Unfortunately we have no clear or detailed record of his thinking at that point on strategic questions.

On the other hand we do know a great deal about the next stage in his activity after he moved with the *Northern Star* from Leeds to London. Already working with Engels, he plunged himself enthusiastically into the London émigré political scene and it was internationalism which proved to be his central contribution to British politics. It threw him into a close association with Marx and Engels, though they were both critical of what they saw as his undiscriminating welcome for European political refugees. Both argued that his engagement across a broad front encompassing proletarian and nationalist revolutionaries was a major obstacle to the building of the former tendency.

Jones remained much closer to Marx and Engels at least for as long as the Chartist movement survived. Coming late to the movement, in 1846, he was too late for the full tide of Owenism and neither was he attracted by Jacobinism. His cultural and educational background was probably nearer to that of Engels than any British Chartist. He was firmly internationalist, at home in the French and German languages, but his first enthusiasm was for O'Connor and the Land Plan. Gaoled in the summer of 1848 as a left radical democrat, he came out as a social democrat. He had firm ideas on both the aims of the movement and its organisational practices. He was instrumental in both the drawing up of the new social programme for the NCA in 1851 and the Labour Parliament in 1854. He firmly believed in the necessity for establishing a sound organisational and financial basis for the movement and the post-1851 NCA has been described as the first British social democratic party. His journalistic endeavours were directed to that goal. *Notes to the People* and the *People's Paper* were strongly orientated towards a working-class audience and though they regularly addressed trade union issues, Jones's forté was international questions such as the Crimean War and the Indian Mutiny. The misfortune for this venture was the shrinking audience in the 1850s for socialist politics as active workers became more and more absorbed in trade unionism, co-operation and a variety of other issues.

Most of the leading figures in the movement were active for relatively short periods or impaired in their activity by imprisonment. Vincent did not really return after his release from gaol, transferring his activity to the temperance movement. Cooper also shifted from militant working-class campaigning to free church religion and liberalism. McDouall appears to have had the clearest understanding of how to build organisation from the bottom. He also demonstrated some of the most advanced thinking on class and Chartism. Twice imprisoned, he had a narrow escape from serious charges in 1848 by running to the Continent, but is presumed to have been lost at sea in the early 1850s.

There was also an impressive cadre of leaders at a local level, courageous, methodical and reliable. Some were prominent at different phases, marked by arrest, persecution and weariness. The talents were rarely, if ever, harnessed together. But there is a sense in which they were always facing new problems in uncharted territory, created by Chartism's peculiar situation as perhaps both the last great cross-class radical campaign and the first mass workers' movement.

The Chartist movement had a number of highly talented leaders but never a really effective collective one where the different talents could be harnessed for the common good. The movement was subject to rapid growth and shrinkage to a considerable extent reflecting dramatic economic fluctuations. Its diverse origins brought sharp difference into the leadership, felt most strongly in the downturns. And especially important was the vigilance and action of the state. Arrest, trial and imprisonment could curb enthusiasm and produce a revaluation of past action. For many this meant a long respite, a move into a different activity, emigration or dropping out of the movement. For only a few does it seem to have meant a period of reflective thought about shortcomings and a return to full activity. The few who did keep going therefore tended to imprint their personality and methods on the movement. O'Connor was one who did, maintaining his energy and following until at least 1848, but at the considerable cost of pursuing a major departure in activity, the Land Plan, which was to fail. Despite the possibility that it might have held together a large chunk of the movement in difficult times, it must equally have sacrificed local political organisation, the presence of which could have made a difference when revival was possible in 1848.

Harney also kept going throughout the period, giving the movement a new internationalist perspective, an activity in London which must have proved invaluable as a means of keeping the ideas alive in the capital in the period of downturn. He showed a capacity to learn positively from experience and was central in giving the movement more ideological coherence in its later stages. With Jones he provided an appropriate leadership for the post-1848 period orientated towards the working class. Their differences were probably exacerbated by a failure to connect with a mass movement of workers. They can hardly be held responsible for that failure.

CHAPTER 7

State Power

Finally we must give due attention to the role of the bourgeoisie and its state in demonstrating consciousness of its class interests and thereby contributing to the development of class consciousness in the working class. The almost exclusively landed ruling class became 'aware' of the presence of potential antagonists, bourgeoisie and proletarians, effectively in the 1790s. Terrifying lessons were on offer as the guillotine fell in Paris and the quasi-bourgeois Jacobin army crushed the Austro-Hungarian Emperor at Valmy. At home Valmy was celebrated in Sheffield[1] and the Corresponding Societies brought thousands of British workers onto the streets: 'You did not shoot us when we were rioting for Church and King ... now we are rioting for a big loaf, we must be shot at and cut up like bacon pigs.'[2] And Protestant and Catholic united, however briefly, in Ireland in 1798.

The lessons *were* learnt: to crush the popular movement and win the middle class were important arms of state policy throughout this period. The years were punctuated by repressive legislation, mass arrests and savage punishments, tempered eventually by a more subtle use of restraining, rather than vengeful, sentences. The problem of overkill was perceived after the mass movements of protest generated by the Tolpuddle Martyrs and the Glasgow Cotton Spinners.

The middle classes were assuaged. Paternalist legislation, designed for stability in earlier times, was swept away in the century's early years, to the advantage of the merchant and entrepreneur. The legislative community – the House of Commons – was opened to the middle class in 1832, though for a generation only a few bourgeois entered its portals. A greedy and opportunistic aristocracy increasingly shared vital interests with the bourgeoisie. From 1832 the Whigs pushed, or conceded, measures. In only 20 years the middle class had gained virtually everything it needed to make the nineteenth century the bourgeois century: a New Poor Law, a Municipal Corporations Act, an urban police force, repeal of the Corn Laws and a Joint Stock Act limiting liability in share dealings. Factory reform, the re-introduction of income tax and the continued ascendancy of the Church of England were a small price to pay.

So the upper classes succeeded in building a protective alliance. At no point was its efficacy tested better than in the Chartist period. Much attention has been given to the government's success in recruiting perhaps 50,000 special constables in London in 1848 to deal with the Kennington Common demonstration on 10 April, somewhat less to the fact that a similar policy in the regional centres of Chartist strength was also successfully implemented.

This middle- and upper-class belligerence started earlier, in the spring of 1839. It seems likely that the allegation that Chartism had no following among agricultural labourers should be qualified somewhat. In the South West, at least, there was a concerted policy to wipe the Chartists out. Armed violence against them by farmers and local worthies took place in Devizes, Bath, Trowbridge and Westbury in 1838–39. The movement there was unable to demonstrate publicly again.

Not that demonstrative support for the government from the middle classes was inevitable. It is instructive that in other circumstances the policy of recruiting specials was much less successful. Much greater reluctance was shown in 1842 when the authorities were faced with massive community involvement in the North during the great strikes.[3] Assurance of active military back-up was sought from a government keen to avoid killings, and martyrs.

However, the degree of accord between ruling and middle classes was a strong base on which to develop a concerted policy of repression. Nonetheless, there was a sense of uncertainty, even panic, about such policy in 1842. The 'smokeless chimneys' had not been Thomas Cooper's only observation upon entering Manchester on 16 August: 'In the streets, there were unmistakable signs of alarm on the part of the authorities. Troops of cavalry were going up and down the principal thoroughfares, accompanied by pieces of artillery, drawn by horses.'[4]

Rolling strikes and mass picketing were pretty unfamiliar modes of dissent for the rulers to deal with. In 1842 the force of law and order was still a pretty blunt instrument. It was suited to dealing summarily with isolated outbursts of dissent but had only limited experience of handling mass movements in industrial areas. The magistracy, carrying initial responsibility, was pretty weak and inclined to be indecisive. If its first appeals for calm were not heeded, and if the local forces at its disposal were small and ineffective, it would appeal for military assistance. This could be answered by the part-time yeomenry consisting of the local gentry, or, via the Home Secretary, by regular soldiers. From the ruling-class standpoint, the 1842 outbreak was a many-headed monster. Local resources were, in the main, thin. The police had only small numbers and apart from the Metropolitan force had little training in crowd control. The Met had been used in 1839 in Birmingham and South Wales, but in the summer of 1842 the London working class was also unruly. Deployment of substantial numbers in the provinces could only be undertaken at the cost of defending London.

Another source of men available to the authorities was the enrolled pensioners: men under 55 years of age retired from active military service. Many lived in local working-class communities but threats to their pensions and accommodation lowered any resistance to service they might have had. They were used in the Potteries offensively and in Manchester as street patrols, but with only modest success.

The military commanders were reluctant to sub-divide their forces. They were fearful of small companies being overwhelmed, as happened at Salter Hebble (Halifax) on 16 August when an escort of prisoners was ambushed and drubbed by a band of Chartists. Billeting them on local communities was also dangerous. They could easily be isolated or subjected to Chartist arguments and disaffect. For a time, then, in the first period of the strike the authorities appear to have been paralysed and indecisive. Queen Victoria certainly thought so. She wrote to the Prime Minister on 17 August:

> She is surprised at the little (or no) opposition to the dreadful riots in the Potteries ... and at the passiveness of the troops. It is all very well to send troops down in numbers, and to publish Proclamations forbidding these meetings, but then they ought to act, and these meetings should be prevented. The Queen thinks everything should be done to apprehend this Cooper, and all the Delegates at Manchester. The magistrates in many places seem to act very laxly.[5]

This was, however, the only real moment of uncertainty in the Chartist period.

The peaks of activity in 1839 and 1842 took place against a background of domestic desperation for masses of working people. But 1848 had a further dimension: the international situation. The government was acutely aware of two contingent problems. First, revolution had broken out in France in February, an event greeted with delirious excitement by much of the British radical movement. The government feared emulation. Second, in the wake of the famine Ireland was in turmoil. With the death of O'Connell and the outspoken support of O'Connor, the Irish and English movements appeared to be drawing closer. With thousands of Irish people in many British cities, the authorities feared the possibility of joint insurrectionary activity.

In a sense these foreign and colonial matters masked differences in the ruling class as all fractions united round the need to defend property. The rulers acted with a degree of precision, on all fronts. The public were prepared for state action by an insistent clamour from the press, both Liberal and Tory. The 'awful' events in Paris and Ireland were constantly linked with the call for the Charter.

The army was in the hands of capable strategists with a surprisingly keen intelligence for the situation on the ground in their areas. The army pensioners stood in the background to take on routine duties. The policy was one of containment by the display of massive force, rather than crude confrontation. The police, whilst still fairly thinly spread across the country, were gaining experience and training in crowd control. They were backed by droves of specials, when necessary, and had already reached that point where their versions of events were instinctively accepted by ministers and middle-class juries. Furthermore, they had new technologies at their disposal. Used for the first time in 1839 in a rather rough and ready way, by 1848 the railway had many new routes and faster trains. It was available for the movement of troops and police. Communications were also aided by the coming of the electric telegraph.

The Bench, wholly representative of the propertied classes, was usually quite crude in its directions to juries whilst making pious references to Britain's liberties and superiority over continental systems. The government, Whig for much of the period, was most illiberal in its determination to contain and dissipate dissent. John Saville points to at least ten acts of Parliament available for the authorities to use against the Chartists in 1848 and still there was a clamour for police and courts to have more. Saville concludes that, 'The English political trials of 1848 were exercises in the miscarriage of justice; the obliteration of reason by prejudice and the subversion of legal principles by partisanship of a virulent order.'[6]

The carefully organised and orchestrated state repression in 1848 was certainly effective in both the short-term sense of obstructing Chartist activity, and in the long term by the demoralisation of the movement's leadership. The vast number of arrests, prosecutions and imprisonments took national and local leadership out of the struggle. For the local leadership it was particularly damaging. By 1848 they were mostly working men with no resources. To be removed from work was a sentence of poverty on their dependants. The sentencing policy was very astute. The conviction of hundreds *for relatively short periods* both beheaded the movement and occasioned little protest from beyond the ranks of the Chartists. Chartism went into decline after the summer of 1848. Proponents of the old game of accounting for the 'failure' of the Chartists should look quite hard at this explanation. The Chartists were crushed by a very well co-ordinated state power. There was no 'softer', more liberal approach, as has been claimed: 'its rise and fall is to be related in the first instance ... to the changing character and policy of the state ...'.[7] The wily direction of Lord John Russell simply managed the repression and did it efficiently, deploying all the resources at his disposal.

CHAPTER 8

Conclusion

By the end of 1848 Chartism as a mass movement capable of mobilising tens of thousands of working people was dead. Ten years later the remaining organisation and its press was also gone. Feargus O'Connor and Peter Murray McDouall were dead. Bronterre O'Brien was still engaged in journalism and wrote poetry, but was chronically sick and was to die in 1864. Thomas Cooper was preaching rationalism and would soon revert to the Christianity of his youth. William Lovett was involved in promoting adult education and, like Henry Vincent, active in temperance affairs. Julian Harney was about to emigrate to America. Ernest Jones carried the torch till the end, when he resumed legal practice, moving politically onto the radical end of liberalism.

As we have seen above, it was the O'Brienites who maintained the thread of socialism, carrying it into the First International and beyond to the revival of social democracy in the 1880s, though Marx and Engels always thought the crude class politics of Chartist workers was closer to real socialism than the theorising of the Owenite tradition: 'In its present form, Socialism can never become the common creed of the working class; it must condescend to return for a moment to the Chartist standpoint.'[1]

For the bulk of Chartists who remained active there were a variety of outlets: trade unionism, co-operation, internationalism, temperance and, in the mid-1860s, agitation for parliamentary reform. In the localities the latter usually meant working with the Liberal Party and, to some extent, that body might be said to have inherited a substantial part of the impulse driving Chartism in working-class communities. It is likely, too, that large numbers of men who had suffered imprisonment were lost completely to the movement on their release, demoralised by their experience. We know that a number of men and their families emigrated to America, either to avoid arrest or to begin a new life after their release. A number of such figures played a part in the young American labour movement, though others took up business and farming.[2] The absence of a movement to return to must have been an important factor for both the disillusioned and the emigrant. This may well also have been important in relation to at least some of the leading figures in the 1850s: 'other' activities may have resulted from disappointment.

It would, however, be wrong to imply that the organisational 'fade out' of Chartism in the 1850s indicated a failure to make a significant impact upon British society. The contrary would be true. In fact the Chartist movement was probably the single most important factor in reshaping political attitudes. This is not to argue the conventional Whiggish view that the Chartist arguments were just part of a typically British long evolutionary process. Ultimately, it was argued, good sense would prevail over prejudice and all Britons would achieve their citizenship incrementally and bloodlessly. If there was any hint that the Charter might have been a means for the middle class to siphon off working-class fury over the New Poor Law it was blown apart by the belligerent mass meetings in the North in 1839, the South Wales Rising and the partial uncovering of insurrectionary plotting in several parts of the country.

The bond between the working class and middle class, formed by mutual grievance, was weakened in the years following the Reform Act. It was severed in those few months of 1839. Despite the traditional *political* terminology of the People's Charter, the movement pinning it to its banners was far from traditional. It had a new social dimension. If not yet socialist, it carried a deeply threatening edge in the accent and rhetoric of many of its speakers. Not only the privileges of aristocracy might be swept away but private property itself. Or that is how it seemed to the new alliance of gentry and bourgeoisie that passed for the ruling order in the provinces. This was especially true of the industrial areas of factory, workshop and mine, where, in the heightened tensions of the struggle, traditional deference was in short supply.

Neither the events of 1842 nor 1848 allayed the fears of the ruling class. In 1842 the mass strike became a reality. Employers could sense their ultimate impotence in the face of this weapon of class struggle. Such anxiety found its voice in William Cooke Taylor's recognition of the working-class presence.

If anything, 1848 was a worse nightmare. The potential power of a workers' movement was frighteningly augmented by the international and colonial dimension. British workers apparently sympathised with the French and the Poles, and English and Irish radicals were seen to be working together. In retrospect we can see just how provisional such manifestations were. But this is beside the point. The ruling class, the aristocracy and its long middle-class tail believed that, from their point of view, the worst was possible. They reacted in the first instance with a battery of restrictive legislation from the Master and Servants Act of 1844 to the Treason-Felony and Aliens Acts of 1848. This was followed by legalised violence against the Chartists and an astonishing eruption of public actions by private citizens of the middle class – both legally sanctioned through special constables and informally through organised or 'spontaneous', sometimes drunken, attacks on assemblies.

This was of course an immediate response to a perceived and, at some level, real threat. After 1848 the movement's downturn gave a breathing space for reflection. The lull in popular politics was probably an immediate result of the character of the 1848 events and especially of the state assault upon the Chartists and the Irish. The failure of European revolution and the accession of 'the man on horseback'[3] in France also made a contribution to the sinking of radical morale. However, the situation had an economic dimension too. The economy recovered from the downturn in 1847 and by the early 1850s the rulers were almost overtaken by hubris. Crucially, skilled working men were beginning to enjoy a sustained period of steady earnings. Trade union organisation, so long marginalised by aggressive employers, was able to establish itself.

A section of upper- and middle-class opinion, always fearing a return to the terrifying days of the recent past, campaigned for modest reform to head off potential protest. Self-help was one such strand, and one which found a ready ear among slightly better off working men. William Lovett was one such advocate. The self-help philosophy fitted well with enterprises like co-operation, the demand for workers' education and warnings about the demon drink. Once such practices and modes of thought were established, a section of the working class might be safely admitted to citizenship.

Actually, though, the masses on the street could still refresh the rulers' memories of 'the other working class'. In 1855, probably the final Chartist-led London demonstration took place against Sunday observance. Over 100,000 turned out. Finally, the storming of Hyde Park on 6 May 1867 in a new suffrage campaign reminded the rulers that 10 April 1848 was merely a battle lost for the workers, not a war won for them.[4] So the Chartists could legitimately claim to have forced the rulers to treat with workers. The relative health of the economy helped to create a balance of class forces favouring the rulers but beneath the political surface of society war continued to be waged throughout this period in the factories and workshops.

Chartism imprinted itself upon British political history to a greater extent than is usually admitted. That is despite its apparent failure in its own time. It did not succeed in forcing its programme upon Parliament. At face value the demands were modest enough. At the time Marx thought the achievement of the suffrage could lead to power for the proletariat. In a sense it is probably true that universal suffrage in 1840 could have given the workers an overwhelming majority. This was a working class as yet relatively untouched by the values of capitalist society, apparently imbibed in the second half of the century. Probably more to the point, the class had not developed a reformist leadership ready to deliver the class's radical impulses to the 'national interest'.

The likely outcome of a workers' parliament in the 1840s was civil war, for the struggle over social questions like the New Poor Law, conditions in the factories, education and the housing question would have quickly passed to the streets. And this possibility was the fundamental problem posed by the Chartists to sympathetic fractions of the ruling class. Victory would probably have required a successful insurrection. Divested of the support of a substantial part of the middle class and petit bourgeoisie, the working class was just not developed to the point where it could do it alone. It did not have an appropriate theory of insurrection in a partially industrialised and urban society, nor the time to develop one. It did not have a party to propagandise such a strategy nor to organise the required cadre. In the National Charter Association such a party was there in embryo, but the class itself was too weak and underdeveloped for it to pose real problems for the rulers. The weakness in the working class was reflected in the strength of the ruling class. Without severe pressure coming from the workers' movement, no reforming segment of the ruling class could emerge to offer a way out of impasse. So the ruling class remained united and with it the bodies of armed men which serviced it.

Nevertheless, the Chartists showed a remarkable courage in the face of adversity. They established a tradition of class struggle in Britain on a scale not seen before. It is true that all sides of the future labour movement were represented in its ranks. However, it is the optimism and rage of the enormous meetings of men, women and children, of the marching columns of South Wales miners and the rolling mass pickets of 1842, with which socialists have continued to identify.

Appendix 1

Marx and Engels and Chartism

Karl Marx and Frederick Engels were both active in British politics in the latter part of the Chartist period, Engels from 1843. They cannot be said to have made much of a contribution to the movement's development, though Engels's work with Harney in the mid-1840s, probably influenced the development of an internationalist tendency. In 1848 both were much more involved in the continental revolutions. Marx arrived to settle in Britain in 1852, writing articles for Chartist publications. By this time the movement was in deep decline. Ernest Jones in particular was influenced by Marx, but by 1858 when the organisation was wound up, he was moving away from Marx's ideas to an accommodation with liberalism.

So, it cannot be argued that Marx and Engels made a substantial contribution to Chartism, but the movement and the society which sired it were absolutely central to the development of their revolutionary socialist project. It was Engels's observation of the English working class, primarily in Manchester in 1843–44, which first made concrete their abstract formulation of the proletariat as the 'universal class'. His book *The Condition of the Working Class in England in 1844*, was the first coherent examination of the proletariat in terms of the politics of class struggle. He witnessed the rapid concentration of workers into large factories and the appearance of workers' residential districts. He wrote:

> If the centralisation of population stimulates and develops the property owning class, it forces the development of the workers yet more rapidly. The workers begin to feel as a class, as a whole; they begin to perceive that, though feeble as individuals, they form a power united; their separation from the bourgeoisie, the development of views peculiar to the workers and corresponding to their position in life, is fostered, the consciousness of oppression awakens, and the workers attain social and political importance. The great cities are the birthplaces of labour movements; in them the workers begin to reflect upon their own condition, and to struggle against it; in them the opposition between bourgeois and proletariat first made itself manifest.[1]

He noted that in the peaks of the struggle the British workers were demonstrating a vigorous independent class consciousness. It was this quality which assisted the formulation of a centrepiece of Marxism, the notion that 'the emancipation of the working classes must be conquered by the working classes themselves'. In the Charter Marx saw universal suffrage as the focus round which dissidence could unite and that its achievement would be a profoundly revolutionary act: 'Universal Suffrage is the equivalent for political power for the working class of England, where the proletariat forms the large majority of the population, where in a long, though underground civil war, it has gained a clear consciousness of its position as a class.'[2]

It is probably true that the achievement of universal suffrage in the 1840s would have required a revolutionary overthrow of the existing power, given the fierce determination of the property holders to maintain their authority. Had such a concession been made short of revolution, it is also possible that workers could have taken power via the ballot box since the rulers had not until that time taken seriously the 'domestication of democracy', a process which came to the fore in the times marked by franchise extension in the 1860s and 1880s.

Although Marx and Engels were aware of divisions within the working class, Engels's first instinct seems to have been to idealise the workers. In 1844 he wrote, 'in how great a measure the English proletariat has succeeded in attaining education is shown especially by the fact that the epoch-making products of modern philosophical, political and poetical literature are read by working men almost exclusively'.[3] The peculiar situation of the Irish and the attitude towards them of English workers was noted. The degradation from which many came made them too easily available as scabs. The remedy lay in the liberating and confidence-building of the struggle combined with regular propaganda. But Marx and Engels did exaggerate the immediate potential of the workers to overthrow bourgeois rule.

Even after the crisis of 1848 Marx retained an unbounded optimism in Chartism leading the English workers to victory, and this was not markedly tempered until almost the point of collapse. With hindsight we can see that the advanced factory sector of the economy was very small, the working class very uneven and the state relatively strong. By the time Chartism left the stage, reformism was still not clearly delineated, though a number of former Chartists were drifting into liberalism.

Fifty years later Engels reassessed the state of the working class, examining his own previous analysis. He wrote:

The French Revolution of 1848 saved the English middle class. The socialistic pronouncements of the victorious French workmen frightened the small middle class of England and disorganised the narrower, but more matter of fact movement of the English working class. At the very moment when Chartism was bound to assert itself in its full strength, it collapsed internally before even it collapsed externally, on the 10 April, 1848. The action of the working class was thrust into the background. The capitalist class triumphed along the whole line.[4]

Appendix 2

Chartism and the Historians

The scale of mass involvement, the movement's pioneering nature and the courage of leading figures, nationally and locally, has generated a massive literature. Commencing with the memoirs of participants, the picture of Chartism has been constructed and reconstructed by each subsequent generation informed by contemporary preoccupations, consciously or not. There are four fairly well known memoirs or accounts by participants: those of R.J. Gammage, Thomas Cooper, G.J. Holyoke and W.E. Adams. Though they were written years after the events, all make a very useful contribution to our knowledge of the movement, though with respect to facts they need to be treated with a degree of caution. Coming from participants, they were also predictably partisan. Gammage's book, particularly, became the received account, caricaturing the contribution of Feargus O'Connor and militant Chartism and colouring subsequent accounts.[1] In recent years several memoirs of activists have been discovered and published or republished. Together the accounts of contemporaries form a very good source of attitudes at the time, though coloured by the writers' subsequent perspective.

The Fabian accounts, struggling to establish a reformist strategy for the labour movement at the end of the nineteenth century, privileged the moral force character of the Chartist movement at the expense of physical force or revolutionary strategies. Events like the Newport Rising were marginalised as foolish adventures, the great mass strike of 1842 as having little to do with the movement, and the leadership of O'Connor as egocentric and destructive. Important here were the intemperate remarks on Chartism by the Webbs in their *History of Trade Unionism,* first published in 1894. Chartism 'was disgraced by the fustian of many of its orators and the political and economic quackery of its pretentious and incompetent leaders whose jealousies and intrigues, by successively excluding all nobler elements, finally brought it to nought'.[2]

A better informed and more comprehensive account was that of Mark Hovell published in 1916, but the same antagonism to the physical force wing, and O'Connor especially, is evident there.[3] A glance at Hovell's sources indicates that he relied a great deal on the Francis Place papers and since his own inclinations were towards moderation in politics he may have swallowed those views uncritically. He is certainly very wary and dismissive of inchoate and unpredictable forces like the unskilled or the Irish, about whom he was extremely vicious. As Dorothy Thompson remarked, 'the Irish immigrants in Hovell's picture always "swarm", and serve mainly as shock troops for that turbulent side of the movement for which Hovell had no sympathy or understanding'.[4] However, his concluding chapter is very sympathetic to Chartism and its results. He places it firmly, and not without some subtlety, in the tradition of British gradualism. Nevertheless, given the limitations of available sources and the absence of much scholarly secondary work, Hovell's book was a considerable achievement. A comprehensive narrative account still eludes Chartist historiography 70 years later.

In 1929, Theodore Rothstein published *From Chartism to Labourism* in which he stated that his essay on Chartism

> was written as far back as 1905, at the height of the first Russian revolution, and had for its object to acquaint the militant Russian working class, then preparing under the leadership of the Bolsheviks for armed insurrection, with its great precursor, the English proletariat engaged in a revolutionary struggle under the Chartist banner, and at the same time to demonstrate, by the example of the contest between the 'moral' and 'physical force' schools of the Chartist Movement, the futility of the Menshevik policy of compromise and opportunism.[5]

Although there were shadings of interpretation, these two positions remained the modes within which Chartist history was written before the Second World War. It is an irony, at first sight perhaps, that the move away from such explicitly political readings of the movement was pioneered by someone so politically engaged as G.D.H. Cole. His volume, *Chartist Portraits*, published in 1941, occupies a rather judicious centrist position between Fabian and Marxist interpretations, drawing out the positive and negative characteristics of the selected national leaders of the movement from both physical and moral force wings. It may be of significance that Cole was researching his work on Chartism at the very moment he was campaigning in the labour movement for the Popular Front.[6]

The Labour landslide in 1945, the onset of the Cold War, the caesura in the communist movement and the experience of the long boom in the Western economies contributed to a radical shift in the political terrain which had considerable repercussions on historical scholarship. Fabianism had effectively conquered the Labour Party and much of the working-class movement. The need to draw on history for sustenance was much reduced. The Cold War and its attendant anti-communism tended to marginalise the Communist Party and also produced a shift away from 'revolutionary

struggle' towards the 'parliamentary road' which also discouraged
interest in 'the lessons of history'. The boom and rising living
standards dampened down political activism in the working class.
The first post-war generation was largely depoliticised. To the
extent that interest in working-class and labour history survived at
all, it was with the outstanding personalities of recent history and
their institutions. It moved from the streets to university lecture
rooms and academic monographs.

Interest in the early struggles of the workers was minimal. There
were few exceptions. Outstanding among them was Reg Groves's
We Shall Rise Again, published in 1949 and sadly never reprinted.
Another was John Saville's essay introducing a collection of the
writings of Ernest Jones[7] which firmly placed Jones as the key
figure shifting radical thought towards socialism. *Chartist Studies*,
edited by Asa Briggs, was published in 1959. The editor assembled
twelve essays, largely on the movement in the localities, all written
by university academics. The studies are still very valuable in their
meticulous uncovering of Chartism's roots in certain regions and
towns. In general all stress the importance of local factors, the
moderation of the movement and the marginal impact of the
physical force elements. J.F.C. Harrison's account of Manchester
Chartism, for example, strongly plays down the connection between
Chartism and the mass strike of 1842, whilst subsequent research
has established the most intimate of relationships between the
two. The only other study of note to come out of the 1950s was
F.C. Mather's *Public Order in the Age of the Chartists* (1959) which
is largely unsympathetic to the movement, but invaluable as an
account of the attitude and conduct of the state towards the Chartists.

The 1960s was a period of social and political upheaval. The
revelations of the horrors of Stalinism, the struggles of colonial
peoples for freedom, the stridency of US imperialism, and the
threat of nuclear war brought dissent to the surface once more.
Mainstream communism lost its grip on young people and new
movements burgeoned in the universities imbued with an anti-
establishment character, demonstrating against the bomb, against
apartheid, the deepening crisis in South-East Asia, the oppression
in Eastern Europe, for democracy on the campus and for women's
liberation. Activism was the order of the day. In identifying with
the oppressed across the world, activism meant mass struggle from
below independent of great leaders and deadening bureaucracies.
These dissenting currents were felt in the academic world and
penetrated historical scholarship revitalising labour and social
history with a number of fresh questions about the character of
movements in the past.

The big shift came in the wake of the publication of E.P.
Thompson's *The Making of the English Working Class* (1963) and

the interest in 'history from the bottom up'. The study of Chartism's regional basis, its secondary leadership and the character of its rank and file added much to an understanding of the movement. Contemporary evidence was accorded central importance in revaluating experience. Chartist newspapers, autobiography and participants' accounts were published in modern reprints.[8] Some path-breaking studies appeared. For example, Robert Sykes's establishment of an unambiguous link between Chartism and trade unionism in south-east Lancashire has convincingly corrected earlier opinion that Chartism had little following among trade unionists[9] The best modern work dealing synoptically with the Chartist movement is Dorothy Thompson's *The Chartists: Popular Politics in the Industrial Revolution* (1984), a book which contains an excellent appendix, recording a comprehensive list of the location and timing of Chartist activity. The class struggle interpretation of the movement is vigorously laid out in *'Perish the Privileged Orders'* (1995 by Mark O'Brien.

A number of outstanding monographs have also appeared, shedding much fresh light on some key events and personalities. James Epstein's biography of Feargus O'Connor does much to redress the negative account transmitted by Gammage, the first historian of the movement in the 1850s. The detailed attention given to the role of the *Northern Star* in acting as an organiser and uniting the movement is of great importance. That such a lively and vital organ could be owned and controlled by O'Connor demands that we look at his performance anew. The book's only handicap is that it stops with the release of O'Connor from prison in 1843. A similar approach to his later career would much enhance our understanding of Chartism's later phases. Raymond Challinor's biography of the Chartist attorney William Prowting Roberts[10] is a fine exposition of the important role played by this tenacious and courageous figure. It is especially good on the separation of middle- and working-class radicalism arising from the development of what he calls 'physical force Toryism' and a working class developing social goals. Jutta Schwarzkopf has produced the first comprehensive account of the role of women in the movement.[11]

Two books published in the 1980s uncover the dramatic story of the South Wales rising of 1839. In *The Last Rising* (1985) David Jones constructs a brilliant portrait of social and political society in South Wales before the rising and carefully sifts the evidence pertaining to the events leading to Newport. Ivor Wilkes produces a veritable tour de force, *South Wales and the Rising of 1839* (1984), covering much of the same ground but with greater passion and justifiable hatred for the forces ranged against the Chartists. Both make absolutely clear that what appeared in the autumn of 1839 was a colossal workers' movement committed to the Charter and demonstrating an emerging proletarian consciousness. *London Chartism: 1838–1848* by David Goodway (1984) is a fine portrait of the capital city and its importance to the movement. Paul Pickering has done a similar job for the northern centre of Manchester. *Chartism and the Chartists in Manchester and Salford* (1995) is quite brilliant at recreating the proletarian culture of the world's greatest industrial city but unfortunately is almost silent on militant activities like the mass strike.

In 1982 Mick Jenkins published *The General Strike of 1842*. Impressive in its detail and powerful in its analysis of the workers' movement and its ruling-class antagonists, he creates a sense of a real class struggle in action. Jenkins confirms beyond any reasonable doubt the widespread involvement of working people and active trade unionists in the fight for the Charter. The events of 1848 have found historians in the 1980s too. John Saville's book, *1848: The British State and the Chartist Movement,* is a masterpiece of historical analysis. It may be seen as the culmination of a life's work on the Chartist movement since he deals in detail with some of the themes he laid out in an impressive essay of 1952, 'Chartism in the Year of Revolution:1848'. The book dissects the thought and action of government, bureaucrats, military and press, demonstrating clearly how the state machine learnt from its experience moulding policy to suit its (usually correct) perceptions of how the Chartists, the Irish or the European revolutionaries were thinking. If it is slightly thinner on the actions and thought of the movement, it is because the primary focus was the machinations of state power.[12] Such deficits are amply made up by Henry Weisser in *April 10th,* a book which, whilst dealing with the state more superficially than does Saville, understands and exposes the heartbeat of the movement and its leadership. Weisser's earlier book, *British Working-Class Movements and Europe* (1975) effectively places the Chartist movement in the context of European radical politics. It is also noteworthy that under Saville's joint editorship, *The Dictionary of Labour Biography* has included many useful entries on Chartist activists, including excellent notes on three working-class leaders of Lancashire Chartism: Richard Pilling (vol. VI), Richard Marsden (vol. VIII) and James Leach (vol. IX).

The most controversial recent work so far produced is that of Gareth Stedman Jones. He argues that 'if the interpretation of the language and politics is freed from a priori social inferences, it then becomes possible to establish a far closer and more precise relationship between ideology and activity than is conveyed in the standard picture of the movement'. Previously accounts of the movement in both the Fabian and Marxist traditions had taken for granted that it was born, peaked and declined in a particular concatenation of social and economic conditions. Meeting such interpretations head on, Stedman Jones depicted a movement created and shaped entirely by ideas, a set of ideas inherited from the traditions and practices of eighteenth-century radicalism. Indeed, Stedman Jones has become a leading figure in a movement of historical enquiry – *the linguistic turn* – which argues for language as an independent variable, and possibly the most important one, in uncovering the meaning of human behaviour in the past. It is significant that such thinking and speculation should come at a time when the imaginative vision of the 1960s was being replaced by resurgent neo-liberalism and conservatism.

Such views have not gone unchallenged. John Foster, Neville Kirk[13] and Clive Behagg[14] have all engaged with Stedman Jones on the field of Chartism, finding him selective in his sources, methodologically unsound and fundamentally more reductionist than any of the materialist historians criticised by him. Kirk particularly shows how a different selection of 'language' from articles and reports of speeches can suggest a very different range of thinking among Chartists, indicating a social and economic caste of mind derivative of a contemporaneous social structure rather than that of eighteenth-century radicalism.

Appendix 3

Brief Biographies

Biographies [A] exist of several participants and are referred to in the text. For some of the major and many of the minor figures, the many-volumed *Dictionary of Labour Biography,* edited by John Saville and Joyce Bellamy, is an excellent source [B]. Also useful are Ray Boston, *British Chartists in America* (Manchester, 1971) [C]; Stephen Roberts, *Radical Politicians and Poets in Early Nineteenth Century Britain* (Lampeter, 1993) [D]; and Paul Pickering, *Chartism and the Chartists in Manchester and Salford* (London, 1995) [E]. To get an impression of the age of the leading participants, whilst active in the Chartist movement, I have given their age in 1840 where possible.

William Benbow (1784–?), shoemaker, b. in the North West, a life-long physical force radical activist in Manchester and London, several times imprisoned. Most celebrated for his pamphlet *Grand National Holiday and Congress of the Productive Classes* (1832), which first formulated the tactic of the general strike. [Age in 1840: 56] [B]

Peter Bussey (1805–69), weaver/publican, b. Yorkshire, physical force activist in Bradford. Member of 1839 Convention. Flew to America after the Newport Rising. Implicated in Bradford 'rising' of 1840. [Age in 1840: 35] [C]

John Collins (–1850) toolmaker and fitter (or shoemaker) in Birmingham, and leader of the working-class wing in that city. Gaoled for seditious libel in 1839. Came out more moderate and collaborated with Lovett on educational reform. No biography to date.

Thomas Cooper (1805–92), shoemaker/schoolmaster, b. Leicester and the outstanding leader of Chartism in that city. In 1842 he moved onto the national stage as a first-rate agitator, lecturer and writer for the cause. Bruised by imprisonment but not bowed, he subsequently moved into Christian preaching. His remains one of the outstanding working-class autobiographies. [Age in 1840: 35] [A, B]

Thomas Ainge Devyr (– c. 1880), radical journalist, b. Donegal, emigrated to London in 1838, moving on to Newcastle in 1839. He quickly became a leader of the insurrectionary wing of the movement in Newcastle and was close to the Winlaton ironworkers. News of the failure at Newport caused him to fight to restrain the armed workers. Fleeing from their ire and the long arm of the state, he escaped to the United States where he edited an anti-slavery journal and wrote a most informative autobiography, *The Odd Book of the Nineteenth Century*. No biography to date.

John Frost (1784–1887), linen draper, b. Newport and associated with radical politics from the late 1790s. Perhaps uneasily thrust into the leadership of the Newport Rising in 1839 but his principled courage never faltered. Sentenced to death, later commuted to transportation, he returned to Wales and a hero's reception in 1855. [Age in 1840: 56] [A]

George Julian Harney (1817–97), b. Deptford. Went to sea as a boy but returned to shore due to ill-health after one voyage, became a shop-boy, and plunged into radical politics as a street seller and journalist for the unstamped press in his teens. He greatly admired the radical Jacobins of revolutionary France, argued for insurrection and suffered several periods in gaol. The most internationalist minded of the Chartist leaders, he associated with Marx and Engels. One of the outstanding touring lecturers as well as editor of the *Northern Star*. [Age in 1840: 23] [A]

Ernest Jones (1819–69), b. Berlin. A bright son of the gentry, he moved to Chartism in his mid-twenties, becoming the outstanding leader of its later phases. Lawyer, lecturer, poet and journalist, he is credited with turning Chartism towards a firmer organisational structure and 'social' democracy, theorising both during his time in prison following 1848. [Age in 1840: 21] [A]

James Leach (1804?–69), handloom weaver?/bookseller, b. Wigan. A central figure in Manchester Chartism and possibly the first advocate of the National Charter Association of which he was an Executive member. An enthusiastic worker for the link between trade unionism and Chartism, a fine agitator and a key figure in arguing for the mass strike in 1842. Despite imprisonment, he remained a leading lecturer for the Chartists throughout the 1840s. [Age in 1840: 36?] [B, E]

William Lovett (1800–77), cabinet-maker, b. Cornwall. Moved to London as a boy. Involved early in artisan educational and militant political activity. Probably the drafter of the People's Charter in

1836, after involvement in campaigns for the unstamped press and co-operation he was gaoled with Collins in 1840. He emerged from prison in 1841 slipping out of the mainstream leadership of the movement and dedicating himself to improving workers' education. [Age in 1840: 40] [A, B]

Robert Lowery (1809–63), seaman/tailor/bookseller, b. North Shields. Radical activist from the early 1830s who saw suffrage as the panacea for working-class problems. A 1839 convention delegate from Newcastle. Held militant views but rapidly moved away from them. Chartist missionary in Scotland, the North East and the South West. Shifted into teetotalism from 1840, his Chartist activity waning. [Age in 1840: 31] [A, B]

Peter Murray McDouall (c. 1815–54), b. Newton Stewart, Wigtownshire. A qualified surgeon practising at Ashton-under-Lyne, he was a tireless agitator speaking at dozens of meetings nationwide in the 1840s. Edited his own paper, *The Chartist and Republican Journal.* Probably the strongest advocate of cementing a connection between Chartism and trade unionism. Lost at sea when emigrating to Australia. [Age in 1840: c. 25] [Biographical essay by Raymond Challinor. See Chapter 3, note 27.]

James Bronterre O'Brien (1804–64), lawyer, b. County Longford, Ireland. Turned early to political journalism, editing the *Poor Man's Guardian.* Probably the most theoretically sophisticated of the leaders focusing attention upon Chartism's need to win the working class. His health seriously damaged by imprisonment, on his release he moved away from an insurrectionary perspective but pioneered social democracy in the radical movement. (Age in 1840: 36] [A]

Feargus O'Connor (1796–1857), farmer/radical journalist, b. County Cork, Ireland. Republican family background. Political activist from the early 1820s. Lived in London from 1833 as an Irish MP (disqualified). Brilliant speaker and agitator travelling thousands of miles and speaking at hundreds of meetings for the cause. Inspired immense loyalty and affection among the working class. Unjustly vilified by some contemporaries, his reputation only recently restored by James Epstein's fine biography. Founded Britain's most successful radical newspaper the *Northern Star* and held the movement together after the state's assault following the mass strike of 1842. (Age in 1840: 44) [A]

Richard Pilling (1799–1874), handloom weaver/ factory operative, b. Bolton district. He was an outstanding working-class political activist engaged in all of the major campaigns of the 1830s in the Manchester district. Imprisoned. Possibly the leading motivator of the 1842 mass strike, firmly establishing the link between Chartism and trade unionism. [Age in 1840: 41] [B]

(R. J.) Reginald John Richardson (1808–61), carpenter/newsagent/ pamphleteer, b. Manchester. Active from the time of Peterloo which he had witnessed as a boy, and 'involved in every movement that has taken place amongst the working classes since I can remember' (RJR 1854). Imprisoned in 1840 where he wrote *The Rights of Women*. Member of the NCA Executive Committee 1841. [Age in 1840: 32] [E]

Henry Vincent (1813–78), composer, b. London, childhood in Hull. Joined London Working Men's Association in 1836. Chartist 'missionary' mainly in Wales and the West Country from 1837. Outstanding orator. Twice imprisoned. Moved from militancy to moderation on release, provoking much hostility in the movement. Founder of Teetotal Chartism. [Age in 1840: 27] [B]

George White (1811–68), woolcomber, b. Cork. Leading figure in Leeds, Bradford and Birmingham movement. Strong physical force activist and leader of the abortive Bradford insurrection in 1848. Served six prison sentences but never bowed to the state. [Age in 1840: 29] [D]

Notes

Chapter One

1 John Britton, *Autobiography*, 1851, cited in Francis D. Klingender, *Art and the Industrial Revolution*, London, 1972, p. 91.
2 Cited in David McNally, *Against the Market*, London, 1993, p. 98.
3 A workers' spokesman, cited in T. Koditschek, *Class Formation and Urban Industrial Society: Bradford, 1750–1850*, Cambridge, 1990, p. 357.
4 Paradoxically Stephens, whilst proclaiming the right and need of the masses to use physical force to achieve their ends, did not support the six points of the Charter, and ultimately after his arrest and imprisonment denounced it. See Thomas Milton Kemnitz, 'J.R. Stephens and the Chartist Movement' *International Review of Social History* (henceforth *IRSH*), 19, 1974.
5 John Foster, *Class Struggle and the Industrial Revolution*, London, 1977, see table pp. 154–9 for Oldham radicals traced in activities *c*. 1830–50.
6 Iain McCalman, *Radical Underworld: Prophets, Revolutionaries, and Pornographers in London, 1795–1840*, Cambridge, 1993, ch. 10.

Chapter Two

1 Argued out in *Past and Present*, 36, 1967, D.J. Rowe for Place and 38, 1967, I. Prothero for Lovett.
2 Edward Thompson's phrase from *The Making of the English Working Class*, London, 1963, p. 517.
3 Caroline of Brunswick, rejected wife of the unpopular Prince Regent, became, in 1820, the unlikely focus of mass radical demonstrations of support, in the wake of the Peterloo Massacre.
4. In 1837 five cotton spinners were brought to trial for murder, illegal conspiracy threats and intimidation during a sixteen-week strike. The charges were soon seen to be false and reduced to intimidation, but the men were still transported for seven years, provoking a massive campaign of protest throughout the industrial areas of Britain. See W.H. Fraser, 'The Glasgow Cotton Spinners', in J. Butt and J.T. Ward, *Scottish Themes*, Edinburgh, 1976, p. 80.
5 See Pat Hollis, introduction to *The Poor Man's Guardian 1831–1835*, London, 1969, and her *Pauper Press: A Study in Working Class Radicalism of the 1830s*, Oxford, 1970.

6 William Lovett (1800–77), a Cornishman, a non-apprenticed cabinet-maker who had arrived in London at 21. See Joel Weiner, *William Lovett*, Manchester, 1989, and Lovett's autobiography, *The Life and Struggles of William Lovett in His Pursuit of Bread, Knowledge and Freedom* (1877), London, 1977.

7 Jennifer Bennett, 'The London Democratic Association', in James Epstein and Dorothy Thompson, eds, *The Chartist Experience: Studies in Working Class Radicalism and Culture, 1830–1860*, London, 1982.

8 Thomas Attwood, cited in Asa Briggs, *Chartist Studies*, London, 1959, pp. 18–19.

9 Foster, *Class Struggle in the Industrial Revolution*, pp. 184–5.

10 Donald Read, 'Chartism in Manchester', in Briggs, *Chartist Studies*, p. 38.

11 David Gadian, 'Class Formation and Class Action in North West Industrial Towns 1830–1850', in R.J. Morris, ed., *Class, Power and Social Structure in British Nineteenth Century Towns*, Leicester, 1986, pp. 28–32 demonstrates how local Chartists were led by middle-class elements at their inception but gradually in the militant phases developed working-class leaderships. He also makes the important point that the social character of leaderships does not necessarily mean middle-class domination. Such leaders might be surrogates for workers who could not risk exposure.

12 R. Sykes, 'Early Chartism and Trade Unionism,' in Epstein and Thompson, eds, *The Chartist Experience*, p. 154.

13 D. Read, *The English Provinces*, Manchester, 1964, p. 44, discusses the numbers on Kersal Moor in September 1838. Read's conservative estimate is of 50,000 but of greater importance than the numbers is the large list of trades participating and the places from which marchers came.

14 John L. Baxter, 'Early Chartism and Labour Class Struggle', in S. Pollard and C. Holmes, eds, *Essays in the Economic and Social History of South Yorkshire*, Sheffield, 1976, pp. 135–58.

15 Ibid., and see F.J. Kaijage, 'Labouring Barnsley 1816–1856: A Social and Economic History', unpublished PhD thesis, University of Warwick, 1975.

16 Thomas Ainge Devyr, *The Odd Book of the Nineteenth Century*, New York, 1882, p. 177.

17 Thomas Milton Kemnitz, 'The Chartist Convention of 1839', *Albion*, 10: 2, 1978. The author shows that 71 delegates sat in the Convention though the maximum sitting at *any one* session was 52.

18 See the marvellous analysis offered by Iorwerth Prothero, 'William Benbow and the Concept of the "General Strike" ', *Past and Present*, 63, 1974.

19 Gwyn A. Williams, *The Merthyr Rising*, London, 1978, p. 77. 'They enforced solidarity through terror, by means of a developed system of warning notes, night meetings, signals by horn. Blacklegs and other offenders were visited by a herd dressed in animal clothes, women's dresses, turn coats led by a horned Bull.'

20 Ivor Wilkes, *South Wales and the Rising of 1839*, Beckenham, 1984, p. 155.

21 Cited in David Jones, *The Last Rising,* Oxford, 1985, p. 49.
22. Ibid., p. 97.
23 The 'Hosts of Rebecca' was a secret society. Its adherents, consisting largely of rural workers, disguised themselves in women's clothes and attacked and destroyed toll gates.
24 Devyr, *Odd Book,* pp. 200–10.
25 A.J. Peacock, *Bradford Chartism 1838–1840,* York, 1969, pp. 40–3 for the detailed story of the spy James Harrison. But also S. Roberts, *Radical Politicians and Poets in Early Victorian Britain,* Lampeter, 1993, p. 59, for an account of the leading figure Robert Peddie.
26 D. Jones, *Chartism and the Chartists,* Appendix II, for the Aims and Rules of the NCA.
27 Ibid., p. 73.

Chapter Three

1 *Manchester Guardian,* 20 August 1842.
2 Benjamin Wilson, *Struggles of an Old Chartist,* Halifax, 1887, in David Vincent, ed., *Testaments of Radicalism: Memoirs of Working Class Politicians 1790–1885,* London, 1977, p. 199.
3 Cited in R. Fyson, 'The Crisis of 1842: Chartism, the Colliers' Strike and the Outbreak in the Potteries', in Epstein and Thompson, eds, *The Chartist Experience.*
4 Adrian Desmond and James Moore, *Darwin,* London, 1991, p. 297. Darwin and his family left London for the Downs. The authors argue that the almost 20-year postponement of publication of *The Origin of Species* is to be explained by Darwin's fear that its publication in the 1840s might have given sustenance to revolutionaries.
5 Mick Jenkins, *The General Strike of 1842,* London, 1980, p. 68.
6 Ibid., p. 83.
7 Stockport had proved to be tough town to crack. A determined committee of the trades fought hard to keep the wages question separate from Chartism. The flying pickets from outside were especially important. T.D.W. Reid and Naomi Reid, 'The 1842 "Plug Plot" in Stockport', *IRSH,* 24, 1979.
8 *Northern Star,* 1 January 1842, p. 6.
9 Richard Pilling, *The Trial of Feargus O'Connor and Fifty Eight Others* (1843), New York, 1970, p. 250.
10 Ibid., p. 250.
11 Lord Macauley, *Hansard,* 3 May 1842.
12 *Northern Star,* Editorial, 14 May 1842, p. 2.
13 Robert Hall, 'Tyranny, Work and Politics: The 1818 Strike Wave in the English Cotton District', *IRSH,* 34, 1989.
14 R. Sykes, 'Physical Force Chartism: The Cotton District and the Chartist Crisis of 1839', *IRSH,* 30, 1985, pp. 229–30.
15 J.R. Cuca, 'Industrial Change and the Progress of Labour in the English Cotton Industry', *IRSH,* 22, 1977, p. 244.
16 *Northern Star,* 16 July 1842.
17 Jenkins, *General Strike,* p. 145.

18 Dorothy Thompson, *The Chartists: Popular Politics in the Industrial Revolution*, London, 1984, p. 284.

19 Richard Otley's defence, in *The Trial of Feargus O'Connor*, p. 246.

20 Richard Pilling's defence, 1843, in *The Trial of Feargus O'Connor*, p. 250.

21 *Trades Journal*, 1 March 1841.

22 *Northern Star*, 5 March 1842.

23 Cited in Jenkins, *General Strike*, p. 140.

24 Ibid., p. 176.

25 A.R. Schoyen, *The Chartist Challenge*, London, 1958, p. 118.

26 *Northern Star*, 22 January 1842, p. 4. The sardonic reference to the 'swinish multitude' comes from Edmund Burke's characterisation of the masses in his *Reflections on the French Revolution* (1791) and was satirically answered by Thomas Paine in *The Rights of Man*, Pt 1, 1791.

27 R. Challinor, 'Peter Murray McDouall and Physical Force Chartism', *International Socialism*, Second Series, 12, 1981, pp. 66–7.

28 Thomas Cooper, *The Life of Thomas Cooper* (1872), Leicester, 1971, p. 192.

29 Ibid., p. 206.

30 Ibid., p. 208.

31 James Leach's testimony, in *The Trial of Feargus O'Connor*, p. 282.

32 William Cooke Taylor, *Notes of a Tour in the Manufacturing Districts of Lancashire* (1842), London, 1968, p. 6.

33 Alexis de Tocqueville, in Christopher Harvie *et al.*, *Industrialisation and Culture 1830–1914*, London, 1975, pp. 40–1.

34 Hsien-Ting Fang, *The Triumph of the Factory System in England*, Tientsin, 1930, p. 146.

35 *Trial of Fergus O'Connor*, p. 97.

36 Cited in F.C. Mather, 'The Government and the Chartists', in Briggs, *Chartist Studies*, p. 390.

37 Jenkins, *General Strike*, pp. 222–4.

38 Ibid., p. 226.

39 Ibid.

40 Ibid., pp. 235–6.

41 Cooke Taylor, *Notes of a Tour*, p. 331.

42 Neville Kirk, *The Growth of Working Class Reformism in Mid Victorian England*, Beckenham, 1985, p. 19.

Chapter Four

1 James Epstein, *The Lion of Freedom*, Beckenham, 1982, p. 86, n. 40. Though, as always, there were many more readers than buyers.

2 Lovett, *Life and Struggles*, p. 254.

3 Brian Harrison, 'Teetotal Chartism', *History*, June 1973.

4 Kirk, *The Growth of Working Class Reformism*, pp. 145–8.

5 Cecil Driver, *Tory Radical: The Life of Richard Oastler*, New York, 1970. Even the modest advance of this act was subverted by many employers through the operation of the 'relay system' used to introduce longer hours and shift work for adults by working children in relays.

6 M. Chase, *The People's Farm*, Oxford, 1988, and John Saville's Introduction to R.G. Gammage, *History of the Chartist Movement*

1837–1854, London, 1969. Saville writes, 'What historians have missed in their analysis of the Land Plan is the flood of discussion and debate concerning land questions during the 1830s and 1840s. The desirability of making allotments and cottage gardens available to agricultural labourers; the advantages and disadvantages of peasant holdings; the merits of spade husbandry compared with field cultivation; the problems of land tenure, organisation and rural social structure – all these matters were actively commented on during these two decades.'

Chapter Five

1   Cited in Schoyen, *Chartist Challenge,* p. 14.
2   Cited in Henry Weisser, *British Working Class Movements and Europe: 1815–1848,* Manchester, 1975, p. 132.
3   See discussion of this point in Henry Weisser, *April 10th,* pp. 288–91.
4   Ibid., pp. 77–8.
5   Ibid., ch. 5.

Chapter Six

1   Thompson, *The Chartists,* Appendix, pp. 341–68.
2   Rachel O'Higgins, 'The Irish Influence in the Chartist Movement', *Past and Present,* 20, 1961, p. 86.
3   Ibid., p. 91.
4   Robert Southey, 1821, cited in J.A. Jackson, *The Irish in Britain,* London, 1963, p. 153.
5   Cited in Thompson, *The Chartists,* p. 135.
6   From 'The Rights of Woman', R.J. Richardson, in D. Thompson, *The Early Chartists,* London, 1971, p. 115.
7   There is the curious story of Howard Morton who wrote exceptionally well informed articles from Manchester for Harney's papers, the *Democratic Review* and *Red Republican.* No such person turns up in any other activity of the movement. It is thought that Morton was actually Marx and Engels's female friend, Helen McFarlance, who translated the *Communist Manifesto.* Discussed in Schoyen, *Chartist Challenge,* pp. 202–3.
8   Gareth Stedman Jones, 'Rethinking Chartism', *Languages of Class,* London, 1982.
9   ' … if the interpretation of the language and politics is freed from a priori social inferences, it then becomes possible to establish a far closer and more precise relationship between ideology and activity than is conveyed in the standard picture of the movement.' Stedman Jones, 'Rethinking Chartism', p. 55.
10   In an important article replying to Stedman Jones, Neville Kirk argues that he would 'defend Chartism as a social, class based movement [and] that … Jones greatly underestimates the influence exerted by economic and social factors [and that] Jones's awful dread of economic reductionism leads not to materialism, but to an unsatisfactory

idealism'. Kirk then goes on to cite numerous examples of quite obviously class-laden language from participants in the movement. 'In Defence of Class', *IRSH*, 32, 1987, p. 5 for quote and subsequent pages for examples.

11 Clive Behagg, turning Jones on his head, insists that, 'we must ascribe a social value to language in context ... Notions of workplace consensus, the ethos of competition, control of production, and democratization were not universal in nature; rather they had, by the 1830s, become avowedly class-specific in their use and application.' C. Behagg, *Politics and Production*, London, 1990, p. 103.

12 As Paul Pickering catalogues in 'Class Without Words: Symbolic Communication in the Chartist Movement', *Past and Present*, 112, 1986, to rely on records of speeches is absurd since reporters butchered them wittingly and unwittingly (a matter repeatedly complained of by contemporaries). He offers an analysis of the significance of dress codes, citing the case of O'Connor who adopted the working man's 'fustian suit' on his release from York Prison (1841), clearly to visibly identify with this constituency.

13 Jenkins, *The General Strike*. The link between the economic and political was first made in Staffordshire in July, and was heard among Scottish miners, and Lancashire cotton operatives in mid-August. 'I hope you men of Hyde will be true to each other then we will soon have our rights; that will be the Charter and nothing but the Charter.'

14 The Newport insurrectionaries of course deserted their worskhops and coal-mines to march on Newport, but in a sense this was incidental, since there is no sense of of their challenging their bosses' property rights. It might be thought that a situation where insurrection was the objective was a situation where such arguments might have surfaced.

15 Thompson, *The Chartists*, p. 65.

16 Epstein, *The Lion of Freedom*. 'The *Northern Star* ... found its way to the Cut side, being subscribed to by my father and five others. Every Sunday morning these subscribers met at our house to hear what prospect there was of the expected smash up taking place. It was my task to read aloud so that all could hear at the same time; and the comments that were made on the events foreshadowed would have been exceedingly edifying to me were I to hear them now.' Ben Brierley, an old Chartist, writing 50 years on.

17 As was his membership of the House of Commons where he fought, virtually alone in the face of anger and derision, for working-class recognition and against the state's repressive measures, especially the Gagging Act of 1848. Weisser, *April 10th*, p. 286.

18 Cited in G.D.H. Cole, *Chartist Portraits*, London, 1941, p. 332.

19 David McNally, in response to Stedman Jones, shows how O'Brien clearly tried to develop a theory going far beyond the alleged eighteenth-century radical limitations of the movement and most tellingly that these *socialist* ideas were regularly expounded in the popular *Poor Man's Guardian* in the first half of the decade which brought Chartism. *Against the Market*, pp. 133–8.

20 Cited in McNally, *Against the Market*, p. 134.

21 Marx and Engels, *Letters to Americans,* New York, 1953, p. 89. Cited in Stan Shipley, *Club Life and Socialism in Mid-Victorian London,* London, 1971, p. 6.

Chapter Seven

1 Gwyn A. Williams, *Artisans and Sans Culottes,* 2nd edn, London, 1989, p. 3.
2 Ibid., p. 100.
3 F.C. Mather, *Public Order in the Age of the Chartists,* Manchester, 1959, p. 84. Shopkeepers, for example, the backbone of the specials, relied on the workers for custom. There is evidence from Stockport of direct shopkeeper support for the strikers. See Reid and Reid, 'The 1842 "Plug Plot" in Stockport'.
4 Cooper, *Life,* pp. 207–8.
5 The Queen to Sir Robert Peel, dated 17 August 1842, cited in Mather, *Public Order,* p. 33–4.
6 John Saville, *1848,* Cambridge, 1987, p. 173.
7 Stedman Jones, *Languages of Class,* p. 178.

Chapter Eight

1 F. Engels, *The Condition of the Working Class in England,* in *Collected Works,* vol. 4, London, 1975, p. 243.
2 Ray Boston, *British Chartists in America,* London and Manchester, 1971. Especially Appendix A.
3 The downturn in the struggle in France culminated in Louis Napoleon's coup d'etat in December 1851.
4 Royden Harrison, *Before the Socialists,* London, 1965, ch. 3.

Appendix One

1 Engels, *Condition...,* p. 148.
2 Karl Marx, 'The Chartists', *Collected Works,* vol. 11, London, 1979, pp. 335–6.
3 Engels, *Condition...,* p. 245.
4 Engels, Preface to English edn, 1892, *Condition...,* p. 39.

Appendix Two

1 R.G. Gammage, *History of the Chartist Movement,* introduction by John Saville, London, 1969.
2 S. and B. Webb, *History of Trade Unions,* London, 1919, pp. 174–5.
3 Mark Hovell, *The Chartist Movement,* Manchester, 1918.
4 D. Thompson, *Outsiders: Class, Gender and Nation,* London, 1993, pp. 103–4.
5 Theodore Rothstein, *From Chartism to Labourism,* London, 1929, p. 1.

6 His extended pamphlet, *The People's Front,* was published in 1937 in the Left Book Club. Here he was arguing for both a political alliance to include the Communist Party and a cross-class alliance bridging the middle class–working class gulf.

7 John Saville, ed., *Ernest Jones: Chartist,* London, 1952.

8 Among the most important are, Gammage, *History of the Chartist Movement;* J.G. Harney's *The Red Republican* and *The Friend of the People,* London, 1966; Ernest Jones, *Notes to the People* (1851), London, 1967; Cooper, *Life;* W.E. Adams, *Memoirs of a Social Atom,* New Jersey, 1967, all with introductions by John Saville; J. Collins and William Lovett, *A New Organisation of the People,* Leicester, 1969; F. O'Connor, *The Trial of Feargus O'Connor Esq., and Fifty Eight Other Chartists on a Charge of Seditious Conspiracy,* New Jersey, 1969; *Robert Lowery, Radical and Chartist,* ed. Brian Harrison and Patricia Hollis, London, 1979; and *Testaments of Radicalism: Memoirs of Working Class Politicians 1790–1885,* ed. David Vincent, London, 1977.

9 Sykes, 'Early Chartism and Trade Unionism'.

10 R. Challinor, *A Radical Lawyer in Victorian England,* London, 1990.

11 J. Schwartzkopf, *Women in the Chartist Movement,* London, 1991.

12 A topic John Saville returned to in *The Consolidation of the Capitalist State 1800–1850,* London, 1994.

13 Kirk, 'In Defence of Class'.

14 Clive Behagg, *Politics and Production in the Early Nineteenth Century,* London, 1990.

Index